PRAYING
successfully

PRAYING
successfully

CHARLES SPURGEON

 *Whitaker House*

Unless otherwise indicated, all Scripture quotations are taken from the *King James Version* (KJV) of the Bible.

Scripture quotations marked (RV) are taken from the *Revised Version* of the Holy Bible.

PRAYING SUCCESSFULLY

ISBN: 0-88368-443-8
Printed in the United States of America
Copyright © 1997 by Whitaker House

Whitaker House
30 Hunt Valley Circle
New Kensington, PA 15068

Library of Congress Cataloging-in-Publication Data

Spurgeon, C. H. (Charles Haddon), 1834–1892.
    Praying successfully / by Charles H. Spurgeon.
      p.   cm.
    ISBN 0-88368-443-8 (trade paper)
    1. Prayer—Christianity. 2. Christian life—Baptist authors.
I. Title.
BV215.S68   1997
248.3'2—dc21   97-30553

4 5 6 7 8 9 10 11 12 13 / 09 08 07 06 05 04 03 02 01

Contents

Chapter 1

David's Prayer in the Cave

A prayer when he was in the cave.
—Psalm 142:1

I like the title given to Psalm 142: "*A prayer when he was in the cave.*" David did pray when he was in the cave. If he had prayed half as much when he was in the palace as he did when he was in the cave, things would have been better for him. But, alas, when he was king, we find him rising from his bed in the evening, looking from the roof of his house, and falling into temptation. If he had been looking up to heaven, if his heart had been in communion with God, he might never have committed that great crime that has so deeply stained his whole character.

"*A prayer when he was in the cave.*" God will hear prayer on the land, on the sea, and even under the sea. I remember someone at a prayer meeting saying so. Somebody else at the prayer meeting was rather astonished and asked, "How would God hear prayer under the sea?" The man said that he was a diver, and he often went down to the bottom of the sea after shipwrecks. He said that he had held communion with God while he had been at work in the depths of the ocean.

Our God is not only the God of the hills, but also of the valleys. He is the God of both land and sea. He heard Jonah when the disobedient prophet was at the roots of the mountains and when *"the earth with her bars"* (Jonah 2:6) seemed to be around him forever. Wherever you work, you can pray. Wherever you lie sick, you can pray. There is no place to which you can be banished that God is not near, and there is no time of day or night that His throne is inaccessible.

"A prayer when he was in the cave." The caves have heard the best prayers. Some birds sing best in cages. Likewise, some of God's people shine brightest in the dark. Many an heir of heaven never prays so well as when he is driven by necessity to pray. Some will sing aloud upon their beds of sickness who hardly ever sang when they were well. Some will sing God's high praises in the fire who did not praise Him as they should have before the trial came. In the furnace of affliction the saints are often seen at their best. If you are in a dark and gloomy situation, if your soul is bowed down, may this become a special time of powerful communion and intercession. May the prayer of the cave be the very best of your prayers!

In this chapter, I will use David's prayer in the cave as a picture of a soul under a deep sense of sin. Secondly, I will use it to represent the condition of a persecuted believer. Thirdly, I will write about how it reveals the condition of a believer who is being prepared for greater honor and wider service.

8

The Person Convicted of Sin

First, let me try to use this psalm as a picture of the condition of a soul under a deep sense of sin.

A little while ago, perhaps, you were out in the open field of the world, sinning nonchalantly, plucking the flowers that grow in those poisoned valleys and enjoying their deadly perfume. You were as happy as your sinful heart could be, for you were giddy and careless and thoughtless. However, it has pleased God to capture you. You have been arrested by Christ and have been put in prison. You are behind bars. You feel like one who has come out of the bright sunshine and balmy air into a dark, musty cavern, where you can see very little, where there is no comfort, and where there appears to be no hope of escape.

Cry to God

Well now, according to the psalm before us, which is meant for you as well as for David, your first business is to make an appeal to God. I know the doubts you may have. I know the fears you may have of God. I know how frightened you may be at the very mention of His name. But if you want to come out of your present gloom, I charge you to go to God at once. See, the psalm begins, *"I cried unto the LORD with my voice; with my voice unto the LORD did I make my supplication"* (Ps. 142:1). Cry to God with your voice. If you have no place where you can use your voice, cry to God in silence, but do cry to Him. Look Godward. If you look in any other direction, all is darkness. Look Godward. There, and only there, is hope.

"I have sinned against God," you say. Be assured that God is ready to pardon. He has provided the great Atonement through which He can justly forgive the greatest offenses. Look Godward, and begin to pray. I have known people to do this who hardly believed in God. Having a faint desire to pray, they cried to God. Even though it was a poor prayer, God heard it. I have known some to cry to God in utter despair. When they hardly believed that there could be any use in praying, still it was that or nothing. They knew that it could not hurt them to pray, and so they got down on their knees and cried. It is wonderful to see what poor prayers God will hear and answer—prayers that have no legs to run with, no hands to grasp with, and very little heart. Still, God has heard them and has accepted them.

Get on your knees, you who feel guilty. Get on your knees if your heart is sighing on account of sin. If the dark gloom of your iniquities is gathering around you, cry to God. He will hear you.

Make a Full Confession

The next thing to do is to pour out your heart. David said, *"I poured out my complaint before him; I showed before him my trouble"* (Ps. 142:2). The human heart longs to express itself. An unuttered grief will lie and smolder in the soul until its black smoke blinds the very eyes of the spirit.

Sometimes it is not a bad thing to speak to a Christian friend about the anguish of your heart. I would not encourage you to make it a priority—far from it—but it may be helpful to some. But I do encourage you to make a full confession unto the Lord.

Tell Him how you have sinned. Tell Him how you have tried to save yourself and have failed. Tell Him what a wretch you are, how fickle, how proud, how unruly. Tell Him how your ambition carries you away like an unbridled horse. Tell Him all your faults, as far as you can remember them. Do not attempt to hide anything from God. You cannot do so, for He knows all. Therefore, do not hesitate to tell Him everything—the darkest secret, the sin you would not even wish to whisper to the evening's breeze. Tell it all. Confession to God is good for the soul. *"Whoso confesseth and forsaketh* [his sins] *shall have mercy"* (Prov. 28:13).

I urge you who are now in a gloomy cave to seek a secret and quiet place and, alone with God, to pour out your heart before Him. David said, *"I showed before him my trouble"* (Ps. 142:2). Do not think that the use of pious words can be of any help. It is not merely words that you have to utter; you have to lay all your trouble before God. As a child tells his mother his griefs, tell the Lord all your griefs, your complaints, your miseries, your fears. Get them all out, and great relief will come to your spirit.

Acknowledge That God Is Your Only Hope

So, first, appeal to God. Secondly, make confession to Him. Thirdly, acknowledge to God that there is no hope for you but in His mercy. Put it as David did: *"I looked on my right hand, and beheld, but there was no man that would know me"* (v. 4). There is only one hope for you; acknowledge that. Perhaps you have been trying to be saved by your good works. They are altogether worthless, even if you

11

heap them together. Possibly you expect to be saved by your religiousness. But half of it is hypocrisy, and how can a person hope to be saved by his hypocrisy? Do you hope to be saved by your feelings? What are your feelings? They are as changeable as the weather. A puff of wind will change all your fine feelings into murmuring and rebellion against God.

Friend, you cannot keep the law of God! Keeping it perfectly is the only other way to heaven besides Christ. The perfect keeping of God's commandments would save you if you had never committed a sin. But, since you have sinned, even that will not save you now, for future obedience will not wipe out past disobedience.

Here, in Christ Jesus, who is the atoning sacrifice for sin, is the only hope for you. Lay hold of it. In the cave of your doubts and fears, where you are chilled and numbed by the clinging dampness of your despair around you and by the dread of the wrath to come, make God in Christ your sole confidence, and you will yet have perfect peace.

Plead with God

Furthermore, if you are still in the cave of doubt and sin, plead with God to set you free. You cannot present a better prayer than the prayer of David in the cave: *"Bring my soul out of prison, that I may praise thy name"* (Ps. 142:7).

If you are in prison, you cannot get out by yourself. You may grab the bars and try to shake them, but they are unmovable. You cannot break them with your hands. You may meditate, think, invent, and devise, but you cannot get through those bars.

However, there is a hand that can cut bars of iron. Oh, prisoner in the iron cage, there is a hand that can open your cage and set you free! You do not have to be a prisoner. You do not have to be confined. You may walk in freedom through Jesus Christ, the Savior. Only trust Him, and believingly pray David's prayer right now: *"Bring my soul out of prison, that I may praise thy name"* (v. 7). He will set you free!

How sinners do praise God's name when they get out of the prison of sin! I remember how, when I was set free, I felt like singing all the time. I understood very well the words of Charles Wesley:

> Oh, for a thousand tongues to sing
> My great Redeemer's praise!

I recall a story that my old friend, Dr. Alexander Fletcher, told some children one time. He said that he was going down the street one day and saw a boy standing on his head, turning cartwheels, and jumping up and down. He said to him, "What are you doing? You seem to be tremendously happy." The boy replied, "Oh, mister, if you had been locked up for six months and had just gotten out, you would be happy, too!"

I have no doubt that this is very true. When a person gets out of the prison of sin—a far worse prison than any earthly prison—he must praise God's free grace and dying love. He must sing and make his whole life musical with the praise of the emancipating Christ.

Now, that is my advice to you who are in a cave because of conviction of sin. May God make that cave a blessing to you! If you are under a sense of sin, heed what I have already said; you do not need to notice anything else that I am going to write in this chapter. If you are not in the cave of conviction, the rest of this chapter belongs to you.

The Persecuted Believer

I will go on to my second subject. This psalm sets forth the condition of a persecuted believer.

A persecuted believer! Are there any in our country? Yes, dear friends, there are many! When a person becomes a Christian, he immediately becomes different from the people around him.

I was standing at my window one day, meditating on possible subjects for my next sermon. I could not decide on a text, when, all of a sudden, I saw a flock of birds. A canary had escaped from its cage and was flying over the roofs of the houses opposite mine. It was being chased by about twenty sparrows, along with other rough birds. Then I thought of that text, *"Mine heritage is unto me as a speckled bird, the birds round about are against her"* (Jer. 12:9). Why, the birds in pursuit seemed to say to one another, "Here is a yellow fellow. We have not seen a bird like him in our city. He has no business here. Let us pull off his bright coat. Let us kill him, or let us make him as dark and dull as we are."

That is just what people of the world try to do to Christians. Here is a godly man who works in a factory, or a Christian woman who is employed in an office building. Such Christians will have a sad tale to tell of how they have been hunted down, ridiculed, and scoffed at by ungodly coworkers.

David's Prayer in the Cave

You Do Not Know What to Do

It may be that you are in the condition just described. You hardly know what to do. You are as David described himself in Psalm 142, for he said, *"My spirit was overwhelmed within me"* (v. 3). Perhaps you are a new believer, and your coworkers have turned against you and become your persecutors. It is a new thing to you as a young believer. You are quite perplexed and completely unsure of what you should do. They are severe, ferocious, and incessant. They find out your tender spots and know just how to touch you on those raw places. You are like a lamb in the midst of wolves; you do not know which way to turn.

Well then, say to the Lord what David said: *"When my spirit was overwhelmed within me, then thou knewest my path"* (v. 3). God knows exactly where you are and what you have to bear. Have confidence that, when you do not know what to do, He can and will direct your way if you trust Him.

You Are Tempted

In addition, it may be that you are greatly tempted. David said, *"They privily laid a snare for me"* (v. 3). This is often the case with a young man. His coworkers find out that he has become a Christian, and they try to trip him up. If they can, they will devise a scheme by which they can make him appear to be guilty, even if he is not. Ah, if you are in this situation, you will need much wisdom! I pray that you may never yield to temptation but may hold your ground by divine grace. Young Christian

15

soldiers often have a very rough time of it in the barracks. But I hope that you will prove yourself a true soldier and not yield an inch to those who would lead you astray.

It will be very painful if, in addition to that, your family turns against you. David said, *"There was no man that would know me"* (Ps. 142:4). Is it the same with you? Are your father and mother against you? Is your wife or your husband against you? Do your brothers and sisters call you a hypocrite? Do they point the finger of scorn at you when you get home? And often, when you go home after church, where you have been so happy, do you have to hear profanity the moment you enter the house?

Christians should pray for young people who are newly converted, for their worst enemies are often those in their own household. "I would not mind so much," a new believer said, "if I had a Christian friend to go to. I spoke to a Christian the other day, and he did not seem to care about my situation at all."

Such a nonchalant attitude really hurts a young convert. Take John as an example. He has truly, lovingly, given his heart to Christ. The manager where he works is a Christian man. John is ridiculed by his coworkers, and he tries to talk to this Christian man about it. John's boss squelches him in a moment and has no sympathy for him. Well, there is another Christian working near John's desk. As the young convert begins to tell him a little about his trouble, this man, too, is very grumpy and cross.

I have noticed that some Christians appear to keep to themselves, and they do not seem to notice the troubles of beginners in the Christian life. Do not let this be the case with you. My dear brothers and sisters, cultivate great love to those who, having come into the army of Christ, are harassed by adversaries. Like David, they are in the cave. Do not disown them. They are trying to do their best. Stand side by side with them. Say to the persecutors of your young Christian friend, "I, too, am a Christian. If you are honoring that young man with your ridicule, let me have my portion of it. If you are pouring contempt on him, give me a share of it, for I also believe as he believes."

Will you do that? Some of my readers will, I am sure. Will you stand by the man of God who upholds the Lord's revealed truth? Some of you will. But there are plenty of people who want to save their skin. If they can sneak away from a fight, they are glad to get home, go to bed, and slumber until the battle is over. May God help us to have more of the lion in us, and not so much of the chicken! May God grant us grace to stand by those who are out-and-out for God and for His Christ, so that we may be remembered with them in the day of His appearing!

You Are Weak

It may be that your worst point is that you feel very feeble. You say, "I would not mind the persecution if I felt strong, but I am so weak." Well now, always distinguish between feeling strong and being strong. The person who feels strong is weak; the person who feels weak is strong. Paul said, *"When I am weak, then am I strong"* (2 Cor. 12:10). David prayed, *"Deliver me from my persecutors; for they are stronger than I"* (Ps. 142:6).

Just hide yourself away in the strength of God. Pray much. Take God for your refuge and your portion. Have faith in Him. Then you will be stronger than your adversaries. They may seem to pull you down, but you will soon be up again. They may set before you puzzles that you cannot solve. They may come up with their scientific knowledge, and you may be at a disadvantage. But never mind that. The God who has led you into the cave will turn the tables for you one of these days. Only hold on, and hold out, even to the end.

I am glad that there is some trouble in being a Christian, for it has become a very common thing to profess to be one. If I am right, it is going to become a much less common thing for a person to say, "I am a Christian." There will come times when sharp lines will be drawn. Some of us will help to draw them if we can. The problem is that people bear the Christian name but act like worldlings and love the amusements and the follies of the world. It is time for a division in the house of the Lord in which those for Christ go into one camp and those against Christ go into the other camp. We have been mixed together too long.

I, for one, say, "May the day soon come when every Christian will have to run the gauntlet!" It will be a good thing for genuine believers. It will just blow some of the chaff away from the wheat. We will have all the purer gold when the fire gets hot and the crucible is put into it, for then the dross will be separated from the precious metal.

Be courageous, my fellow believer. If you are now in the cave, the Lord will bring you out of it in His own good time.

The Believer in Training

Now, to close this chapter, I want to write a little about the condition of a believer who is being prepared for greater honor and wider service.

Is it not a curious thing that whenever God means to make a man great, He always breaks him in pieces first? There was a man whom the Lord meant to make into a prince. How did He do it? Why, He met him one night and wrestled with him! We always hear about Jacob's wrestling. Well, I dare say Jacob did wrestle, but it was not Jacob who was the principal wrestler: *"There wrestled a man with him until the breaking of the day"* (Gen. 32:24). God wrestled with him. He touched the hollow of Jacob's thigh and put it out of joint before He called him Israel, which means "a prince of God." The purpose of the wrestling was to take all of Jacob's strength out of him. When his strength was gone, then God called him a prince.

Now, David was to be king over all of Israel. What was the way to Jerusalem for David? What was the way to the throne? Well, he went by way of the cave of Adullam. He had to go there first and be an outcast, for that was the way by which he would be made king.

Have you ever noticed that whenever God is about to give you a promotion, elevating you to a larger sphere of service or a higher platform of spiritual life, you always get thrown down? That is His usual method of working. He makes you hungry before He feeds you. He strips you before He clothes you. He makes you nothing before He makes you something. This was the case with David. He was to

19

be king in Jerusalem, but he had to go to the throne by way of the cave.

Now, are you about to go to heaven or to a more heavenly state of sanctification or to a greater sphere of usefulness? Do not be surprised if you go by way of the cave. Why is this? God wants to teach you several things.

Pray

First, in order for God to make you greatly useful, He must teach you how to pray. The man who is a great preacher and yet cannot pray will come to a bad end. A woman who is noted for her Bible teaching and yet cannot pray will also come to a bad end. If you can be great without prayer, your greatness will be your ruin. If God means to bless you greatly, He will make you pray greatly, as He did with David, who said while in the cave, *"I cried unto the LORD with my voice; with my voice unto the LORD did I make my supplication"* (Ps. 142:1).

Always Believe in God

The person whom God will greatly honor must always believe in God, even when he is at his wit's end. *"When my spirit was overwhelmed within me, then thou knewest my path"* (v. 3). Are you never at your wit's end? Then God has not sent you to do business in great waters. If He has, before long you will be in a great storm, staggering to and fro and at your wit's end. Oh, it is easy to trust when you can trust yourself. But when you cannot trust yourself, when your spirit sinks below zero in the chill of utter despair, then it is time to trust in God. If that is your case, you have the marks of a believer who can lead God's people and be a comforter to others.

Stand Alone

Next, on the way to greater usefulness, many a man or woman of God must be taught to stand alone. *"I looked on my right hand, and beheld, but there was no man that would know me"* (Ps. 142:4). If you want others to help you, you will make a decent follower. But if you look to no man and can stand alone, God being your Helper, you will make a good leader.

It was an impressive thing when Martin Luther stepped out of the ranks of Rome. There were many good men around him who said, "Be quiet, Martin. You will be burned at the stake if you do not hold your tongue. Let us stay where we are, in the Church of Rome, even if we have to hear false teaching. We can believe the Gospel and still remain where we are." But Luther knew that he had to defy antichrists and declare the pure Gospel of the blessed God. He knew he had to stand alone for the truth, even if there were as many devils against him as there were tiles on the housetops in his hometown of Worms, Germany.

That is the kind of man whom God blesses. I fervently desire that many young people reading this book will have the courage to say, "I can stand alone if need be. I would be glad to have my coworkers and friends and family stand with me, but if nobody will go to heaven with me, I will say good-bye to them and go to heaven alone through the grace of God's dear Son."

Delight in God

The person whom God will bless will be the person who delights in God alone. David said, *"I cried unto thee, O LORD: I said, Thou art my refuge and my portion in the land of the living"* (Ps. 142:5).

Oh, to have God as our refuge and to make God our portion! You may lose your job. You may lose your income. You may lose the approval of others. "But," says the believer, "I will not lose my portion, for God is my portion. He is my job, my income, my everything. I will hold onto Him, come what may."

If you have learned to *"delight thyself also in the LORD,"* then *"he shall give thee the desires of thine heart"* (Ps. 37:4). Then you are in a state in which God can use you and make much of you. But until you make much of God, He will never make much of you. May God deliver us from having our portion in this life, for if we do, we are not among His people at all!

Sympathize

The person whom God will use must be taught to sympathize with hurting Christians. David said, *"I am brought very low"* (Ps. 142:6).

If the Lord means to bless you, believer, and to make you useful in His church, you can be sure that He will try you. Half, perhaps up to ninety percent, of a minister's trials are not sent to him for his own welfare; they are sent for the good of other people. Many children of God who go very smoothly to heaven do very little for others. But others of the Lord's children, who have experienced all the ups and downs and changes of mature believers' lives, have done so only so that they may be better equipped to help others. They are able to weep with those who weep or rejoice with those who rejoice.

Therefore, you, my brother who has entered the cave, and you, my sister who has deep spiritual challenges, I want to comfort you by showing you that this is God's way of making something out of you. He is digging you out. You are like an old ditch that cannot hold any more, and God is digging you out to make room for more grace. His shovel will cut sharply as it digs up clump after clump and throws them aside. The very thing you would like to keep will be thrown away, and you will be hollowed out and dug out so that the word of Elisha may be fulfilled: *"Make this valley full of ditches. For thus saith the LORD, Ye shall not see wind, neither shall ye see rain; yet that valley shall be filled with water"* (2 Kings 3:16–17). You are to be tried, my friend, so that God may be glorified in you.

Praise

Lastly, if God means to use you, you must be full of praise. Listen to what David said: *"Bring my soul out of prison, that I may praise thy name: the righteous shall compass me about; for thou shalt deal bountifully with me"* (Ps. 142:7).

If God is trying you in order to benefit you and afflicting you in order to promote you, may He give you grace to begin to praise Him! The singers are the ones who go before the others; those who can praise the best will be fit to lead others in the work. Do not ask me to follow a gloomy leader. Do not ask me to march to a sad tune. No, no, give me a joyous song. Sing unto the Lord who has triumphed gloriously (Exod. 15:1). Praise His great name again and again.

If you have a cheerful spirit, if you are glad in the Lord and joyful after all your trials and afflictions, and if you rejoice all the more because you have been brought low, then God is making something out of you. He will yet use you to lead His people to greater works of grace.

Encouragement

What I have written in this chapter I have written to three kinds of people: those convicted of sin, persecuted believers, and disciples in training. May God grant to each of you the grace to know which you are and to take what belongs to you!

If you know anyone who is in a cave, stop and comfort him. Even if you feel that you are too busy, put yourself second. Just paddle your own canoe alongside someone else's little ship, and see whether you cannot communicate with the poor troubled one on board. Say a word to cheer a sad heart. Always do this. If you are in prison yourself, the way out of it is to help another out. God restored the riches of Job when he prayed for his friends. When we begin to look after others and seek to help others, God will bless us. May it be so, for His name's sake!

Chapter 2

Ask and Have

*Ye lust, and have not: ye kill, and desire to have,
and cannot obtain: ye fight and war, yet ye have not,
because ye ask not. Ye ask, and receive not, because ye
ask amiss, that ye may consume it upon your lusts.*
—*James 4:2–3*

May these striking words of our text above
be made profitable to us by the teaching of
the Holy Spirit.

Man is a creature abounding in wants. He is
ever restless. His heart is full of desires. I can hardly
imagine a person who does not have many desires of
some kind or another. Man is like a sea anemone
with its multitude of tentacles, which are always
hunting in the water for food. Man is like certain
plants that send out tendrils, seeking to climb
higher. Man steers for what he thinks to be his port,
but, as yet, he is tossed about upon the waves. One
of these days he hopes to find his heart's delight, and
so he continues to desire with more or less expectancy.

This fact applies to both the worst of people and the best of people, but there is a difference between the desires of sinners and the desires of saints. Sinners' desires become lusts; their longings are selfish, sensual, and consequently evil. The current of their desires runs forcefully in a wrong direction. These lusts, in many cases, become extremely intense. They make the man their slave and domineer over his judgment; they stir him up to violence. He fights and wars, perhaps he literally kills. In God's sight, who considers anger to be the same as murder (Matt. 5:21–22), he kills quite often. His desires are so strong that they are commonly referred to as passions. When these passions are fully excited, the man himself struggles vehemently. Like the kingdom of heaven, the kingdom of the Devil suffers violence, and the violent take it by force (Matt. 11:12).

At the same time, there are desires in Christians also. To rob the saints of their desires would be to injure them greatly, for by their desires they rise out of their lower selves. Believers desire the best things: things that are pure and peaceful, admirable and elevating. They desire God's glory; therefore, their motives are higher than the motives that inflame the unrenewed mind. Such desires in Christians are frequently very fervent and forceful. Indeed, they should always be so. Desires from the Spirit of God stir the renewed nature, exciting and stimulating it. They make the believer groan in anguish until he can attain the things that God has taught him to long for.

The lusts of the wicked and the holy desires of the righteous have their own ways of seeking gratification. The wicked seek to satisfy their lusts through contention. They kill and desire to have; they fight and war. On the other hand, the desires of the righteous, when properly guided, take a far better course to achieve their purposes. They express themselves in fervent and persistent prayer. The godly man, when full of desire, asks and receives from the hand of God.

At this time I will, by God's help, try to explain our text, James 4:2–3. First, I will explain the poverty of lusting, expressed in the words, *"Ye lust, and have not."* Next, I will show the poverty that many professing Christians have in spiritual things. They also long for things and do not have them. In the third place, I will write on the wealth with which holy desires are rewarded if we simply use the right means. If we ask, we will receive.

The Poverty of Lusting

First, consider the poverty of lusting. *"Ye lust, and have not."* Carnal lusts, however strong they may be, often do not obtain what they seek. The text says, *"Ye...desire to have, and cannot obtain."* The carnal person longs to be happy, but he is not. He yearns to be great, but he grows more contemptible every day. He aspires after this and after that, whatever he thinks will content him, but he is still not satisfied. He is like the troubled sea that cannot rest. One way or another, his life is a disappointment. His labors are vexatious and in vain; they are only fuel for the fire. How can it be otherwise? If we sow the wind, must we not reap the whirlwind, and nothing else (Hos. 8:7)?

Even if the strong lusts of an active, talented, persevering person do give him what he seeks, how soon he loses it. He has it, then he does not have it. The pursuit is toilsome, but the possession is a dream. He sits down to eat, and, behold, the feast is snatched away; the cup vanishes when it is at his lips. He wins to lose. He builds, but the sandy foundation slips from under his tower, and it lies in ruins. Take Napoleon as an example. He conquered kingdoms but died discontented on a lonely island in the middle of the ocean. As Jonah's protecting plant withered in a night, so empires have fallen suddenly, and their lords have died in exile. What people obtain by warring and fighting is an estate with a short lease. The possession is so temporary that it still stands true, "[They] *lust, and have not.*"

Even if such a person has enough talent and power to retain what he has won, in another sense he does not have it even while he has it, for the pleasure that he looked for in it is not there. He plucks the apple, and it turns out to be one of those Dead Sea apples that crumble to pieces in the hand. Such a person may be rich, but God takes from him the power to enjoy his wealth. By his lusts and his wars, the lustful person at last obtains the object of his cravings. However, after a moment's gratification, he loathes that which he so passionately lusted for. He longs for the tempting pleasure, seizes it, and crushes it by his eager grasp.

See the boy hunting the butterfly, which flits from flower to flower while he pursues it eagerly. At last it is within reach, and with his cap he knocks it down. But when he picks up the poor remains, he finds the painted butterfly spoiled by the act that won it. Likewise, it may be said of multitudes of people, *"Ye lust, and have not."*

Ask and Have

James set forth their threefold poverty: *"Ye kill, and desire to have, and cannot obtain"*; *"Ye have not, because ye ask not"*; and, *"Ye ask, and receive not, because ye ask amiss."*

Fighting to Get Ahead

The lustful *"kill, and desire to have, and cannot obtain."* If they fail, it is not because they did not work to gain what they wanted. For, according to their nature, they used the most practical means within their reach, and used them eagerly, too. According to the mind of the flesh, the only way to obtain a thing is to fight for it. In fact, James set this down as the reason for all fighting: *"From whence come wars and fightings among you? come they not hence, even of your lusts that war in your members?"* (James 4:1). But their fighting is unsuccessful, for James said in the next verse, *"Ye fight and war, yet ye have not."* Yet, people cling to this method from age to age.

We are told that if a person is to get along in this world, he must contend with his neighbors and push them from their place of advantage. He must not be concerned about his neighbor's success, but he must mind his own opportunities. He must be sure to rise, no matter how many he may trample on. He cannot expect to get ahead if he loves his neighbor as himself. It is a fair fight, and every man must look out for himself. Do you think I am being sarcastic? I am, but I have heard this sort of talk from people who truly meant it. So they take to fighting, and their fighting is often victorious, for according to the text they *"kill"*—that is, they over-throw their adversary and make an end of him.

Multitudes of people are living for themselves, competing here and warring there, fighting for their own welfare with the utmost perseverance. Conscience is not allowed to interfere in their transactions. The old advice rings in their ears, "Get money; get money honestly if you can, but by any means get money." It does not matter that body and soul are ruined and that others are deluged with misery. They must fight on, for there is no discharge in this war. James wisely said, *"Ye kill, and desire to have, and cannot obtain: ye fight and war, yet ye have not."*

Refusing to Ask

When people who have their hearts set on their selfish desires do not succeed, they may possibly hear that the reason of their failure is *"because* [they] *ask not."* Is success to be achieved by asking then? The text seems to hint this, and the righteous find that it is so.

Why does the person with intense desires not try asking? The reason is, first, that it is unnatural to the natural man to pray. He would just as naturally sprout wings and fly. He despises the idea of supplication. "Pray?" he asks. "No, I want to work. I cannot waste time on devotions. Prayers are not practical; I want to fight my way. While you are praying, I will have beaten my opponent. I go to my office and leave you to your Bibles and your prayers."

The carnal person has no intention of asking God for anything. He is so proud that he considers himself to be his own providence. He thinks that his own strong arm will get him the victory. When he is very liberal in his views, he admits that though he does not pray, there may be some good in it, for it quiets people's minds and makes them more comfortable. But, as far as any prayer ever being answered, he scoffs at the idea. He talks philosophically and theologically about the absurdity of supposing that God alters His conduct to answer prayers. "Ridiculous," he says, "utterly ridiculous!" Therefore, in his own great wisdom he returns to his fighting and his warring, for by such means he hopes to achieve his goal. Yet he does not obtain it. The whole history of mankind shows that evil lusts fail to obtain their object.

Futile Asking

For a while the carnal person goes on fighting and warring, but eventually he changes his mind, for he is ill or frightened. His purpose is the same, but if it cannot be achieved one way, he will try another. If he must ask, well, he will ask. He will become religious and do good to himself in that way. He finds that some religious people prosper in the world and that even sincere Christians are by no means fools in business. Therefore, he will try their plan.

Now he comes under the third reprimand of our text: *"Ye ask, and receive not."* Why does the lustful person not obtain his desire, even when he resorts to asking? The reason is that his asking is a mere matter of form; his heart is not in his worship. He buys a book containing what are called forms of prayer, and he repeats these. He has discovered that repeating is easier than praying, and it demands no thought.

I have no objection to your using a form of prayer if you pray with it; but I know a great many who do not pray with it, but only repeat the words. Imagine what our families would be like if, instead of our children speaking to us frankly when they need something, they always went to the library to hunt up a prayer to read to us. Surely there would be an end of all family feelings and love. Life would be shackled in its movements. Our households would become a kind of boarding school or barracks. All would be ritual and formality, instead of happy eyes looking up with loving trust into fond eyes that delight to respond. Many spiritual people use a form, but carnal people are almost sure to do so, for they are only interested in the form, not in true prayer.

If your desires are the longings of fallen nature, if your desires begin and end with your own self, and if the primary purpose for which you live is not to glorify God but to glorify yourself, then you may fight, but you will not have. You may get up early and stay up late, but nothing worth gaining will come of it. Remember how the Lord has spoken in the book of Psalms:

> *Cease from anger, and forsake wrath: fret not thyself in any wise to do evil....For yet a little while, and the wicked shall not be: yea, thou shalt diligently consider his place, and it shall not be. But the meek shall inherit the earth; and shall delight themselves in the abundance of peace.* (Ps. 37:8, 10–11)

I believe I have written enough to prove the poverty of lusting.

Spiritual Poverty

Secondly, I have before me a serious business, and that is to show how Christian churches may suffer spiritual poverty. They, too, may desire to have and not be able to obtain. Of course, the Christian seeks higher things than the worldly person, or else he would not be worthy of the name "Christian." Outwardly, at least, his objective is to obtain the true riches and to glorify God in spirit and in truth. But look, dear believers—all churches do not get what they desire. Not here and there, but in many places, churches are nearly asleep and are gradually declining.

They find excuses, of course. They say that the population is dwindling or that another place of worship is attracting the people. There is always an excuse handy when a person needs one. However, we must face the facts: public worship is almost deserted in some places, the ministry has no rallying power, members who put in an appearance are discontented or indifferent, and in such churches there are no conversions. What is the reason for these things?

Christian Competition

First, even professed Christians may pursue desirable things by a wrong method. *"Ye fight and war, yet ye have not."* Have not churches tried to prosper by competing with other churches? We foolishly say, "At such and such a place of worship, they have a very clever minister; we must get a clever minister, too. In fact, he must be a little cleverer than the other church's hero. That is just what we need—a clever minister!" How awful that we should live in an age in which we talk about clever ministers preaching the Gospel of Jesus Christ! How sad that this holy service should be thought to depend on human cleverness!

Churches have competed with each other in architecture, music, apparel, and social status. In some cases, there is a measure of bitterness in the rivalry. It is not pleasant to small minds to see other churches prospering more than their own. Other congregations may be more earnest than we are, they may be doing God's work better, but we are too apt to turn a jealous eye toward them. We would rather they did not get along quite so well. *"Do ye think that the scripture saith in vain, The spirit that dwelleth in us lusteth to envy?"* (James 4:5). If there were a disturbance among them that caused the church to break up and die, we would not rejoice. Of course not. But neither would we suffer any real sorrow.

In some churches an evil spirit lingers. God will never bless such means and such a spirit. Those who give way to them will desire to have but will never obtain.

Failure to Ask

Meanwhile, what is the reason that these churches do not have a blessing? The text says, *"Because ye ask not."* I am afraid there are churches that do not ask. Prayer in all forms is too much neglected. Private prayer is allowed to decay. I will put it to the conscience of every reader to determine how much he attends to secret prayer and how much time he spends with God in secret fellowship. Certainly the healthy existence of secret prayer is vital to church prosperity. Family prayer is easier to judge, for we can see it. I fear that in these days many have quite given up family devotions. I pray you do not imitate such people.

I hope you have the same attitude as a certain Scottish laborer. He obtained employment in the house of a wealthy farmer who was known to pay well, and all his friends envied him because he had gone to live in such a place. However, in a short time he returned to his native village. When they asked him why he had left his job, he replied, "I cannot live in a house that has no roof." The rich man's house had a physical roof, of course; but the laborer was speaking of a covering of prayer. A house without prayer is a house without a roof. We cannot expect blessings on our churches if we have none on our families.

As for the attendance at what we call our prayer meetings, is there not a decline? In many cases the prayer meeting is despised. It is looked down on as a sort of second-rate gathering. Some church members are never present, and it does not even prick their consciences that they do not attend. Some congregations combine the prayer meeting with a Bible study so that they can hold only one service during the week.

The other day I read an excuse for all this: people are better at home, attending to family concerns. This is foolish talk. None of us wishes to see people neglect their domestic concerns. However, the people who take care of their own concerns best are the people who are diligent to get everything in order so that they may go to church. Negligence of the house of God is often an indication of negligence of one's own house. If a person does not bring his children to church services, I am persuaded that he is not bringing them to Christ.

Anyhow, the prayers of the church measure its prosperity. If we restrain prayer, we restrain the blessing. Our true success as churches can only be had by asking the Lord for it. Are we not prepared to reform and improve in this matter? Oh, for Zion's travailing hour to come, when an agony of prayer will move the whole body of the faithful!

Praying Improperly

Some may reply, "We have prayer meetings, and we do ask for the blessing, yet it does not come." Is not the explanation to be found in the next verse of the text: *"Ye ask, and receive not, because ye ask amiss"*? When prayer meetings become a mere formality, when believers stand up and waste time with their long orations instead of speaking to God in earnest and burning words, when there is no expectation of a blessing, when the prayer is cold and icy, then nothing is accomplished. He who prays without fervency does not pray at all. We cannot commune with God, who is a consuming fire (Deut. 4:24), if there is no fire in our prayers.

Many prayers fail to achieve their purpose because there is no faith behind them. Prayers that are filled with doubt are requests for refusal. Imagine that you wrote to a friend and said, "Dear friend, I am in great trouble. I am telling you this, and I am asking for your help, because it seems right to do so. But though I am writing to you, I do not believe you will send me any help. Indeed, I would be shocked if you did, and I would speak of it as a great wonder."

Do you think you would get any help? I should say that your friend would be sensible enough to observe how little confidence you had in him. He would reply that, since you did not expect anything, he would not astonish you. Your opinion of his generosity is so low that he does not feel inclined to go out of his way on your account. When our prayers are like that letter, we must not be surprised if we *"receive not,"* for we *"ask amiss."*

Moreover, if our praying is a mere asking that our church may prosper because we want to glory in its prosperity, if we want to see our own denomination largely increased and its respectability improved so that we may share in the honors, then our desires are nothing but lusts after all. How can it be that the children of God manifest the same jealousies and ambitions as people of the world? Should religious work be a matter of rivalry and contest? No. The prayers that seek selfish success will have no acceptance at the mercy seat, no matter how earnest and believing they may be. God will not listen to us but will tell us to leave, for He does not care for petitions in which self is the object. *"Ye have not, because ye ask not...*[or] *because ye ask amiss."*

Your Available Wealth

Now, I have much more pleasant work to do, which is to hint at the wealth that awaits the use of the right means, namely, proper praying.

I invite your most earnest attention to this matter, for it is vitally important. Upon first observation, we find how very small this demand is that God makes of us. Ask? Why, it is the least thing He can possibly expect of us. And it is no more than we ordinarily require of those who need help from us. We expect a poor person to ask. If he does not, we lay the blame for his lack on him.

If God will give for the asking but we remain poor, who is to blame? Is not our blame most grievous? Does it not look as if we are out of touch with God when we will not even ask a favor of Him? Surely there must be in our hearts a lurking enmity toward Him. Otherwise, instead of prayer being an unwelcome necessity, it would be a great delight.

My fellow believers, whether we like it or not, asking is the rule of the kingdom. *"Ask, and ye shall receive"* (John 16:24). It is a rule that never will be altered in anybody's case. Our Lord Jesus Christ is the elder brother of the family, but God did not relax the rule even for Him. Jehovah said to His own Son, *"Ask of me, and I shall give thee the heathen for thine inheritance, and the uttermost parts of the earth for thy possession"* (Ps. 2:8). If the royal, divine Son of God was not exempt from the rule of asking, you and I cannot expect the rule to be relaxed for us.

God blessed Elijah and sent rain on Israel, but Elijah had to pray for it. If the chosen nation was to prosper, Samuel had to plead for it. If the Jews were to be delivered, Daniel had to intercede. God blessed Paul, and the nations were converted through him, but Paul had to pray. Pray he did, *"without ceasing"* (1 Thess. 5:17). His epistles show that he expected nothing except by asking for it.

Moreover, even the most shallow thinker knows that there are some things necessary for the church of God that we cannot get any other way than by prayer. You can get that clever minister I wrote about earlier, and that new church, and that new organ and choir. You can even get them without prayer. However, you cannot get the heavenly anointing without prayer. The gift of God is not to be purchased with money.

Some of the members of a small village church thought that they would build their congregation by hanging a very handsome chandelier in the meetinghouse. Indeed, the villagers talked about this chandelier, and some went to see it, but the light of it soon grew dim.

You can buy all sorts of fancy furniture, you can purchase any kind of paint, brass, and fine linen, together with flutes, organs, and all kinds of instruments. You can get these without prayer. In fact, it would be disrespectful to pray about such rubbish. But you cannot get the Holy Spirit without prayer. Like the wind, He goes where He wishes. He will not be brought near by any process or method apart from asking. Furthermore, there are no mechanical means that will make up for His absence. Prayer is the great door of spiritual blessing, and if you close it, you shut out His favor.

The Privilege of Prayer

Beloved believers, do you not think that this asking that God requires is a very great privilege? Suppose there were a law passed that you must not pray. That would be a hardship indeed. If prayer were to interrupt rather than increase the stream of blessing, it would be a sad calamity.

Have you ever seen a mute person very excited or suffering great pain and, therefore, wanting desperately to speak? It is a terrible sight to see. The face is distorted; the body is fearfully agitated. The mute writhes in dire distress. Every limb is contorted with a desire to help the tongue, but it cannot break its bonds. Hollow sounds come from the breast, and ineffective stutterings awaken some attention, although they cannot reach as far as articulated words. The poor creature is in unspeakable pain.

Suppose our spiritual nature were full of strong desires, yet we were unable to pray. I think it would be one of the worst afflictions that could possibly befall us. We would be terribly maimed and dismembered, and our agony would be overwhelming. Blessed be His name, the Lord ordains a way of expression, and He bids our hearts to speak to Him.

Beloved, we must pray. It seems to me that it ought to be the first thing we ever think of doing when in need. If people were right with God and loved Him truly, they would pray as naturally as they breathe. I hope some of us are right with God and do not need to be driven to prayer. I hope prayer has become an instinct for some of us.

Recently I was told a story about a little German boy. The dear little child believed his God, and he delighted in prayer. His schoolteacher had urged the students to be at school on time, and this child always tried to be. But his parents were leisurely people. One morning, through their fault alone, he had just left the door as the clock struck the hour for school to open. A friend standing nearby heard the little one cry, "Dear God, please help me to be on time for school." It struck the friend that for once prayer could not be heard, for the child had quite a walk ahead of him, and the hour had already come. He was curious to see the result.

Now, it so happened that on this particular morning, the teacher, in trying to open the classroom door, turned the key the wrong way. The lock was stuck, and they had to send for a locksmith to open the door. It was the needed delay! Just as the door opened, our little friend entered with the rest of the children, all in good time.

God has many ways of granting right desires. It was most natural that, instead of crying and whining, a child who really loved God should speak to Him about his trouble. Should it not be natural to us to spontaneously and immediately tell the Lord our sorrows and ask for help? Should this not be the first resort, instead of the last?

Alas, according to Scripture and observation, and I grieve to add, according to my own experience, prayer is often the last resort. Look at the sick man in Psalm 107. Friends bring him various foods, but his soul *"abhorreth all manner of meat"* (v. 18). The physicians do what they can to heal him, but he grows worse and worse. He draws *"near unto the gates of death"* (v. 18). Finally, he cries to the Lord in his trouble (v. 19). He put last what he should have put first.

"Send for the doctor. Prepare him nourishment. Wrap him in blankets!" All very well, but when will you pray to God? God will be called on when the case grows desperate.

Look at the sailors described in the same psalm. Their ship is very close to being wrecked. *"They mount up to the heaven, they go down again to the depths: their soul is melted because of trouble"* (Ps. 107:26). Still they do all they can to ride out the storm. But when *"they reel to and fro, and stagger like a drunken man, and are at their wit's end,"* then *"they cry unto the LORD in their trouble"* (vv. 27–28).

Oh yes, we seek God when we are driven into a corner and are ready to perish. What a mercy that He hears such delayed prayers and delivers the suppliants out of their troubles! But should it be this way with you and with me and with churches of Christ? Should not the first impulse of a declining church be to say, "Let us pray day and night until the Lord blesses us. Let us meet together *'with one accord in one place'* (Acts 2:1) and never separate until the blessing descends on us"?

Prayers Abundantly Answered

Do you know, believers, what great things are to be had for the asking? Have you ever thought about it? Does it not motivate you to pray fervently? All of heaven lies within the grasp of the asking individual. All the promises of God are rich and inexhaustible, and their fulfillment is to be had by prayer. Jesus said, *"All things are delivered unto me of my Father"* (Matt. 11:27), and Paul said, *"All things are yours ...and ye are Christ's"* (1 Cor. 3:21, 23). Who would not pray when all things are handed over to us like this? Promises that were first made to specific individuals are also made to us if we know how to plead them in prayer. For example, only Jacob was present at Peniel, yet Hosea used the word *us* in referring to the experience: *"There he spake with us"* (Hos. 12:4). Israel went through the Red Sea ages ago, yet the word *we* is used in the sixty-sixth Psalm: *"There did we rejoice in him"* (v. 6).

When Paul wanted to give us a great promise for times of need, he used these words: *"For he hath said, I will never leave thee, nor forsake thee"* (Heb. 13:5). Where did Paul get that verse? It was the assurance that the Lord gave to Joshua: *"I will not fail thee, nor forsake thee"* (Josh. 1:5). You may think, "Surely the promise was for Joshua only." No, it is for us. *"No prophecy of the scripture is of any private interpretation"* (2 Pet. 1:20). All Scripture is ours.

See how God appeared to Solomon at night and said, *"Ask what I shall give thee"* (1 Kings 3:5). Solomon asked for wisdom. "Oh, that is Solomon," you say. Read this: *"If any of you lack wisdom, let him ask of God"* (James 1:5). In addition, God gave Solomon wealth and fame in the bargain. Is that unique to Solomon? No, for it is said of true wisdom, *"Length of days is in her right hand; and in her left hand riches and honour"* (Prov. 3:16). This is very similar to our Savior's promise: *"Seek ye first the kingdom of God, and his righteousness; and all these things shall be added unto you"* (Matt. 6:33).

Do you see that the Lord's promises have many fulfillments? They are waiting now to pour their treasures into the lap of those who pray. God is willing to repeat the biographies of His saints in us. He is waiting to be gracious and to load us with His benefits (Ps. 68:19). Does this not lift prayer up to a high level?

Here is another truth that ought to make us pray: If we ask, God will give us much more than we ask. When God promised Abraham that He would give him a child through Sarah, Abraham asked God to bless Ishmael: *"O that Ishmael might live before thee!"* (Gen. 17:18). Abraham thought, "Surely this is the promised child. I cannot expect that Sarah will bear a child in her old age. God has promised me a child, and surely it must be this child of Hagar. *'O that Ishmael might live before thee.'"* God granted him that, but He gave him Isaac as well, and all the blessings of the covenant.

Then there was Jacob. When he knelt down at Bethel to pray, he asked the Lord to give him food to eat and clothes to put on as he continued on his journey. But what did his God give him? When he came back to Bethel several years later, his family and possessions were divided into two large groups. He had thousands of sheep and camels, as well as much wealth. God had heard him and had done immeasurably more than he had asked.

David said of himself, "[The king] *asked life of thee, and thou gavest it him, even length of days for ever and ever"* (Ps. 21:4). Yes, God gave him not only length of days himself, but a throne for his sons throughout all generations. When God told David that his throne would be established forever, he went and sat before the Lord, overpowered with the Lord's goodness.

"Well," you may be saying, "did this concept of getting more than we ask work for New Testament believers?" Yes, it also worked for New Testament suppliants, whether saints or sinners. When a paralytic was brought to Jesus for Him to heal, Jesus said, *"Son...thy sins be forgiven thee"* (Matt. 9:2). The man had not asked for forgiveness, had he? No, but God gives greater things than we ask for!

Hear that poor dying thief's humble prayer, *"Lord, remember me when thou comest into thy kingdom"* (Luke 23:42). Jesus replied, *"To day shalt thou be with me in paradise"* (v. 43). He had not dreamed of such an honor.

Even the story of the Prodigal Son teaches us about God's abundant giving. The Prodigal Son had resolved to say, "I *'am no more worthy to be called thy son; make me as one of thy hired servants'* (Luke 15:19)." What was his father's answer?

> *Bring forth the best robe, and put it on him; and put a ring on his hand, and shoes on his feet...for this my son was dead, and is alive again.* (Luke 15:22, 24)

Get into the position of a petitioner, and you will have what you never asked for and never thought of. People often misquote Ephesians 3:20. They say, "God *'is able to do exceeding abundantly above all that we* [can] *ask or think.'"* The truth is that we *could* ask for the very greatest of things, if we were only more alert and had more faith. Ephesians 3:20 really says that God *"is able to do exceeding abundantly above all that we* [do] *ask or think."* God is willing to give us infinitely more than we actually do ask.

John's Picture of Prayer

I believe that God's church could have inconceivable blessings at this moment if she were only

45

ready to pray. Did you ever notice that wonderful portrayal of prayer in the eighth chapter of the book of Revelation? It is worthy of careful notice.

As John was receiving the remarkable vision of the last times, God gave him this special picture of prayer. It begins in this way: *"When* [the Lord] *had opened the seventh seal, there was silence in heaven about the space of half an hour"* (Rev. 8:1). There was silence in heaven. There were no anthems, no hallelujahs; not an angel stirred a wing. Silence in heaven! Can you imagine it? Then seven angels stood before God, and to them were given seven trumpets. There they waited, trumpet in hand, but there was not a sound. Not a single note of cheer or warning during an interval that was long enough to provoke lively emotion, but short enough to prevent impatience. Silence unbroken, profound, awe-inspiring, reigned in heaven. Action was suspended in heaven, the center of all activity.

"And another angel came and stood at the altar, having a golden censer" (v. 3). There he stood, but no offering was presented. Everything had come to a standstill. What could possibly set it in motion? Prayer could. Prayer was presented together with the merit of the Lord Jesus:

> *And there was given unto him much incense, that he should offer it with the prayers of all saints upon the golden altar which was before the throne.* (Rev. 8:3)

Now, notice what happened. *"And the smoke of the incense, which came with the prayers of the saints, ascended up before God out of the angel's hand"* (v. 4). Prayer was the key to the whole matter. Now the angel began to work.

> *And the angel took the censer, and filled it*
> *with fire of the altar, and cast it into the earth;*
> *and there were voices, and thunderings, and*
> *lightnings, and an earthquake. And the seven*
> *angels which had the seven trumpets prepared*
> *themselves to sound.* (Rev. 8:5–6)

Everything was now moving. As soon as the prayers of the saints were mixed with the incense of Christ's eternal merit and began to ascend from the altar, then prayer became effective. Down fell the living coals among the people on earth. The angels of divine providence, who had stood still before, blew their trumpets. The will of the Lord was done.

Such is the scene in heaven, to a certain degree, even today. Bring the incense! Bring the prayers of the saints! Set them on fire with Christ's merits. On the golden altar let them smoke before the Most High. Then we will see the Lord at work. The will of the Lord will *"be done in earth, as it is in heaven"* (Matt. 6:10).

May God send His blessing with these words, for Christ's sake.

Chapter 3

Real Prayer

*Call upon me in the day of trouble: I will
deliver thee, and thou shalt glorify me.*
—Psalm 50:15

One book charmed me when I was a boy. *Robinson Crusoe* was a wealth of wonders to me. I could have read it twenty times and never grown tired of it. I am not ashamed to confess that I can read it even now with ever fresh delight.

Robinson and his trusted aide Friday, though mere inventions of fiction, are wonderfully real to me, and to many who have read their story. But why am I going on and on about a work of fiction? Is this subject altogether out of place? I hope not. A passage in that book comes vividly to my mind as I contemplate our text, and in it I find more than an excuse to write on this subject.

Robinson Crusoe had been shipwrecked. All alone on a desert island, he was in a very miserable condition. He went to bed and was afflicted with a fever. This fever lasted a long time, and he had no one to help him—no one even to bring him a drink of cold water. He was ready to die.

He was accustomed to sin and had all the vices of an evil sailor, but his hard case caused him to think. Opening a Bible that he had found in his sea chest, he stumbled upon this passage: *"Call upon me in the day of trouble: I will deliver thee, and thou shalt glorify me."* That night he prayed for the first time in his life, and ever after that, he had a hope in God.

Daniel Defoe, the author of the book, was a Presbyterian minister. Though not overly spiritual, he knew enough of faith to be able to describe very vividly the experience of a person who is in despair but finds peace by casting himself upon God. As a novelist, he had a keen eye for the probable, and he could think of no passage more likely to impress a poor broken spirit than this. Instinctively, he perceived the wealth of comfort that lies within the words of Psalm 50:15.

Now I know I have your attention, and that is one reason that I began the chapter this way. But I have a further purpose. Although Robinson Crusoe was not a real person, nor was Friday either, there may be some reader very much like him, a person who has suffered shipwreck in life and has now become a drifting, solitary creature. He remembers better days, but by his sins he has become a castaway for whom no one seeks. He is reading this book, washed up on shore without a friend, suffering in body and crushed in spirit. In a city full of people, he does not have a friend. There is no one who would wish to admit that he has ever known him. He has come to the bare bones of existence now. Nothing lies before him but poverty, misery, and death.

The Lord says to you, my friend, *"Call upon me in the day of trouble: I will deliver thee, and thou shalt glorify me."* I have the feeling that I am writing directly, God helping me, to some poor burdened spirit. Of what use is comfort to those who are not in distress? The words of this chapter will be of no help and may have little interest to those who have no distress of heart. But, however badly I may write, those hearts that need the cheering assurance of a gracious God will dance for joy. Sad hearts will be enabled to receive assurance as it shines forth in this golden text: *"Call upon me in the day of trouble: I will deliver thee, and thou shalt glorify me."*

It is a text that I want to write in stars across the sky or proclaim with the blowing of a trumpet from the top of every tower. It should be known and read by all mankind.

Four important concepts suggest themselves to me. May the Holy Spirit bless what I am able to write about them!

Being Real before God

My first observation is not so much in my text alone as it is in the context. The observation is this: God prefers realism to ritualism. If you will carefully read the entire psalm, you will see that the Lord is speaking of the rituals and ceremonies of Israel. He is showing that He cares little about formalities of worship when the heart is absent from them. Here are several key verses that illustrate this:

> *I will not reprove thee for thy sacrifices or thy burnt offerings, to have been continually before me. I will take no bullock out of thy house, nor he goats out of thy folds. For every beast of the*

> *forest is mine, and the cattle upon a thousand
> hills. I know all the fowls of the mountains:
> and the wild beasts of the field are mine. If I
> were hungry, I would not tell thee: for the
> world is mine, and the fulness thereof. Will I
> eat the flesh of bulls, or drink the blood of
> goats? Offer unto God thanksgiving; and pay
> thy vows unto the most High: and call upon
> me in the day of trouble: I will deliver thee,
> and thou shalt glorify me.*   *(Ps. 50:8–15)*

Thus, praise and prayer are accepted in preference
to every form of offering that the Jew could possibly
present before the Lord. Why is this?

Real Prayer Has Meaning

First of all, real prayer is far better than mere
ritual because there is meaning in it. When grace is
absent, there is no meaning in ritual. It is as sense-
less as a fool's game.

Did you ever stand in a Roman Catholic cathe-
dral and watch the daily service, especially if it happened to be on a holiday? With the boys in white,
and the men in violet, pink, red, or black, there are
enough performers to entertain a city. There are
those who carry candlesticks, those who carry
crosses, those who carry cushions and books, those
who ring bells, those who sprinkle water, those who
bob their heads, and those who bow their knees. The
whole scene is very strange to look at—very amaz-
ing, very amusing, very childish. One wonders, when
he sees it, what it is all about, and what kind of people are really made better by it. One wonders also

what an idea Roman Catholics must have of God if they imagine that He is pleased with such performances. Do you not wonder how the Lord endures it? What must His glorious mind think of it all?

The glorious God cares nothing for pomp and show. But when you call upon Him in the day of trouble and ask Him to deliver you, there is meaning in your groan of anguish. This is no empty formality. There is heart in it, is there not? There is meaning in the sorrowful appeal. Therefore, God prefers the prayer of a broken heart to the finest service that was ever performed by priests and choirs.

Real Prayer Has Spiritual Life

Why does God prefer realism to ritualism? It is for this reason also: There is something spiritual in the cry of a troubled heart. *"God is a Spirit: and they that worship him must worship him in spirit and in truth"* (John 4:24). Suppose I were to repeat the finest creed that was ever composed by learned and orthodox men. Yet, if I had no faith in it, and you had none, what would be the use of repeating the words? There is nothing spiritual in mere orthodox statements if we have no real belief in them. We might as well repeat the alphabet and call it devotion. If I were to burst forth in the grandest hallelujah that was ever uttered by mortal lips, but I did not mean it, there would be nothing spiritual in it, and it would mean nothing to God.

However, when a poor soul gets away into his bedroom and bows his knee and cries, "God be merciful to me! God save me! God help me in this day of trouble!" there is spiritual life in such a cry.

Therefore, God approves it and answers it. Spiritual worship is what He wants, and He will have it or have nothing. John 4:24 uses the word *must*: *"They that worship him must worship him in spirit and in truth."* He has abolished the ceremonial law, destroyed the one altar at Jerusalem, burned the temple, abolished the Aaronic priesthood, and ended forever all ritualistic performance. He seeks only true worshipers, who worship Him in spirit and in truth.

Real Prayer Recognizes God

Furthermore, the Lord loves the cry of the broken heart because it distinctly recognizes Him as the living God, truly sought after in prayer. From much of outward devotion God is absent. But how we mock God when we do not discern Him as present and do not come near to the Lord Himself! When the heart or the mind or the soul breaks through itself to get to its God, then God is glorified. But He is not glorified when we merely perform ritualistic exercises and forget about Him. Oh, how real God is to a person who is perishing and feels that only God can save him! He truly believes that God exists, or else he would not make so passionate a prayer to Him. When he said his prayers before, he cared little whether God heard or not. But he genuinely prays now, and God's hearing is his chief concern.

Real Prayer Has Sincerity

In addition, dear friends, God takes great delight in our crying to Him in the day of trouble because there is sincerity in it. I am afraid that in the hour of our mirth and in the day of our prosperity, many of our prayers and our thanksgivings are hypocrisy. Too many of us are like spinning tops—we do not move into action unless we are whipped. Certainly we pray with deep intensity when we get into deep trouble.

Take, for instance, a man who is very poor. He has lost his job. He has worn out his shoes in trying to find work. He does not know where the next meal is coming from for his children. If he prays in this situation, it is likely to be a very sincere prayer. He would be in real earnest because of real trouble.

I have sometimes wished that very comfortable Christians, who seem to treat religion as if it were a bed of roses, could have just a little time of "roughing it" and really come into actual difficulties. A life of ease breeds hosts of falsehoods and pretenses, which would soon vanish in the presence of matter-of-fact trials.

Many a man has been converted to God by hunger, weariness, and loneliness, who, when he was a wealthy man, surrounded by frivolous flatterers, never thought of God at all. Many a man on board a ship out on the ocean has learned to pray in the cold chill of an iceberg, or in the horrors of a tidal wave out of which the ship could not rise. When the mast has gone by the board and every timber has been strained and the ship has seemed doomed, then hearts have begun to pray in sincerity.

God loves sincerity. When we mean it; when the soul melts in prayer; when we say, "I must have it or be lost"; when it is no sham, no vain performance, but a real heartbreaking, agonizing cry, then God accepts it. That is why He says, *"Call upon me in the day of trouble.*" Such a cry is the kind of worship that He cares for, because there is sincerity in it, and this is acceptable with the God of truth.

Real Prayer Has Humility

Furthermore, in the cry of the troubled one, there is humility. We may go through a highly brilliant performance of religion, following the rites of some showy church—or we may go through our own rites, which may be as simple as they can be—and we may all the while be saying to ourselves, "This is very nicely done." The preacher may be thinking, "Am I not preaching well?" The believer at the prayer meeting may think within himself, "How delightfully fluent I am!" Whenever there is that attitude in us, God cannot accept our worship. Worship is not acceptable if it is devoid of humility.

On the other hand, when a person goes to God in the day of trouble and says, "Lord, help me! I cannot help myself, but do intervene for me," there is humility in that confession and cry. Therefore, the Lord takes delight in that prayer.

Real Prayer Has Faith

The Lord loves such pleadings because there is a measure of faith in them. When the person in trouble cries, "Lord, deliver me!" he is looking away from himself. You see, he is driven out of himself because of the despair in his life. He cannot find hope or help on earth, and therefore he looks toward heaven.

God loves to discover even a shadow of faith in an unbelieving person. God can spy out even a small trace of faith, and He can and will accept prayer for the sake of that little faith.

Oh, dear heart, what is your condition? Are you torn with anguish? Are you sorely distressed? Are you lonely? Are you pushed aside? Then cry to God. No one else can help you. He is your only hope. Wonderful hope! Cry to Him, for He can help you. I tell you, in that cry of yours will be the pure and true worship that God desires. He desires a sincere cry far more than the slaughter of ten thousand rams or the pouring out of rivers of oil (Mic. 6:7). We undoubtedly find in Scripture that the groan of a burdened spirit is among the sweetest sounds that are ever heard by the ear of the Most High. Woeful cries are anthems with Him, to whom all mere arrangements of sound must be like child's play.

See then, poor, weeping, and distracted ones, that it is not ritualism, it is not the performance of pompous ceremonies, it is not bowing and struggling, it is not using sacred words, but it is crying to God in the hour of trouble that is the most acceptable sacrifice your spirit can bring before the throne of God.

How to Take Advantage of Adversity

I now come to my second observation. In our text, *"Call upon me in the day of trouble: I will deliver thee,"* we have adversity turned into advantage. What a wonderful truth! May God impress it on us all!

I write this with all reverence: God Himself cannot deliver a person who is not in trouble. Therefore, it is to some advantage to be in distress, because God can then deliver you. Even Jesus Christ, the Healer of men, cannot heal a person who is not sick. Therefore, sickness is not an adversity for us, but rather an advantageous opportunity for Christ to heal us.

The point is, my reader, your adversity may prove your advantage by offering occasion for the display of divine grace. It is wise to learn the art of making lemonade out of lemons, and the text teaches us how to do that. It shows how trouble can become gain. When you are in adversity, then call upon God, and you will experience a deliverance that will be a richer and sweeter experience for your soul than if you had never known trouble. It is an art and a science to make gains out of losses, and advantages out of adversities.

Now, let me suppose that there is someone among my readers who is in trouble—perhaps another deserted Robinson Crusoe. I am not idly supposing that there is a tried individual among my readership; I know there is.

Well now, when you pray—and, oh, I wish you would pray now—do you not see what a basis for prayer you have? First, you have a basis in the very time you are in: *"the day of trouble."* You can plead, "Lord, this is a day of trouble! I am in great affliction, and my case is urgent!" Then state what your trouble is—a sick wife, a dying child, a bankrupt business, your failing health, or poverty staring you in the face. Say unto the Lord of mercy, "My Lord, if ever a person was in a day of trouble, I am. Therefore, I take the liberty and license to pray to You now because You have said, *'Call upon me in the day of trouble.'* This is the hour that You have appointed for appealing to You: this dark, stormy day. If ever

there were a person who had a right to pray according to Your own Word, I do, for I am in trouble.
Therefore, I will make use of the very time I am in
as a plea with You. Do, I entreat You, hear Your ser-
vant's cry in this midnight hour."

Furthermore, turn your adversity into advantage by pleading God's command. You can go to the
Lord now, at this precise instant, and say, "Lord, do
hear me, for You have commanded me to pray! I,
though I am evil, would not tell someone to ask me
for something if I intended to deny him. I would not
urge him to ask for help if I meant to refuse it."

Do you not know, friends, that we often impute
to the Lord conduct that we would be ashamed of in
ourselves? This must not be. Suppose you said to a
poor person, "You are in very sad circumstances.
Write to me tomorrow, and I will help you." If he did
write to you, you would not treat his letter with contempt. You would be bound to consider his case.
When you told him to write, you meant that you
would help him if you could. And when God tells you
to call upon Him, He does not mock you. He means
that He will deal kindly with you.

I do not know who you are, but you may call upon
the Lord, for He bids you to call. If you do call upon
Him, you can put this argument into your prayer:

> Lord, Thou hast bid me seek Thy face,
>   And shall I seek in vain?
> And shall the ear of sovereign grace
>   Be deaf when I complain?

So, plead the time, plead the trouble, and plead
the command. Then, plead God's own character.

Speak with Him reverently, but believingly, in this fashion: "Lord, it is You Yourself to whom I appeal. You have said, *'Call upon me.'* If my neighbor would tell me to do so, I might fear that perhaps he would change his mind and not hear me. But You are too great and too good to change. Lord, by Your truth and by Your faithfulness, by Your immutability and by Your love, I, a poor sinner, heartbroken and crushed, call upon You in the day of trouble! Oh, help me, and help me soon, or else I will die!"

Surely you who are in trouble have many and mighty pleas. You are on firm ground with the God of the covenant, and you may bravely seize the blessing. I do not feel as if the text is encouraging me half as much as it will encourage those of my readers who are in trouble. Although I thank God that I am full of joy and rest right now, I am half inclined to see if I can dig up a little bit of trouble for myself. Surely if I were in trouble, I would open my mouth and drink in this text. I would pray like David or Elijah or Daniel with the power of this promise: *"Call upon me in the day of trouble: I will deliver thee, and thou shalt glorify me."*

Oh, you troubled ones, leap up at the sound of this promise! Believe it. Let it go down into your souls. *"The LORD looseth the prisoners"* (Ps. 146:7). He has come to loose you.

I can see my Master arrayed in His silk garments. His countenance is as joyous as heaven, His face is as bright as a morning without clouds, and in His hand He holds a silver key. "Where are you going, my Master, with that silver key of Yours?" I ask. "I go," He says, "to open the door of the captive and to loosen everyone who is bound."

Blessed Master, fulfill Your errand, but do not pass by the prisoners of hope! We will not hinder You for a moment, but do not forget these mourners! Go to the heart of every reader, and set free the prisoners of despair. Make their hearts sing for joy by delivering them in the day of trouble after they have called upon You. Because of Your merciful deliverance, they will glorify You!

God Promises Grace

My third topic, God's vow, is clearly found in our text, Psalm 50:15. Here we have free grace vowed to us.

Nothing in heaven or earth can be freer than grace. In our wonderful text God's grace is promised by a vow or covenant. Listen to God's definite promise to deliver us: *"Call upon me in the day of trouble: I will deliver thee."*

If a person once says to you, "I will," you hold him to his promise. He has placed himself at the command of his own declaration. If he is a true man and has plainly said, "I will," you have him in your hand. He was free before giving the promise, but he is not free after giving it. He has put himself in a certain position, and he must act according to what he has promised. Is this not true?

With the deepest reverence, I say the same things about my Lord and Master. He has bound Himself in the text with cords that He will not break. He must now hear and help those who call upon Him in the day of trouble. He has solemnly promised, and He will fully perform His vow.

Notice that our text is unconditional in that it applies to everyone. It contains the gist of another promise that we will discuss in the next chapter: *"Whosoever shall call upon the name of the Lord shall be saved"* (Rom. 10:13).

Remarkably, Psalm 50:15 was originally written to those who had mocked God. They had presented their sacrifices without a true heart. Yet, the Lord said to each of them, *"Call upon me in the day of trouble: I will deliver thee."*

I gather from this that God excludes none from the promise. You atheist, you blasphemer, you immoral and impure one, if you call upon the Lord now, in the day of your trouble, He will deliver you! Come and try Him.

Do you say, "If there is a God"? I declare that there is a God. Come, put Him to the test and see. He says, *"Call upon me in the day of trouble: I will deliver thee."* Will you not test Him now and find Him true? Come here, you enslaved ones, and see if He does not free you! Come to Christ, all of you who labor and are burdened down, and He will give you rest (Matt. 11:28)! In both temporal and spiritual things, but especially in spiritual things, call upon Him in the day of trouble, and He will deliver you.

Moreover, notice that this *"I will"* includes all the power that may be required for deliverance. *"Call upon me in the day of trouble: I will deliver thee."* "But how can this be?" one cries. Ah, that I cannot tell you, and I do not feel bound to tell you. It rests with the Lord to find suitable ways and means. God says, *"I will."* Let Him do it in His own way. If He says, *"I will,"* you can be sure that He will keep His word. If it is necessary to shake heaven and earth, He will do it. He cannot lack power, and He certainly does not lack honesty. An honest man will keep his word at all costs, and so will our faithful God. Hear Him say, *"I will deliver thee,"* and ask no more questions.

I do not suppose that Daniel knew how God would deliver him out of the den of lions. I do not suppose that Joseph knew how he would be delivered out of prison when his master's wife had slandered his character so shamefully. I do not suppose that these ancient believers even dreamed of the way of the Lord's deliverance. They just left themselves in God's hands. They rested on God, and He delivered them in the best possible manner. He will do the same for you. Simply call upon Him, and then *"stand still, and see the salvation of the LORD"* (Exod. 14:13).

Notice, the text does not say exactly when God will bring deliverance. *"I will deliver thee"* is plain enough, but whether it will be tomorrow or next week or next year is not so clear. You are in a great hurry, but the Lord is not. Your trial may not have yet worked all the good for you that it was sent to do, and therefore it must last longer. When the gold is cast into the refiner's fire, it might cry to the goldsmith, "Let me out." "No," he says, "you have not yet lost your dross. You must wait in the fire until I have purified you."

God may likewise subject us to many trials. Yet, if He says, *"I will deliver thee,"* you can be sure that He will keep His word. When you get God's *"I will,"* you may always cash it by faith. God's promise for the future is a bona fide offer for the present, if you simply have faith to use it. *"Call upon me in the day of trouble: I will deliver thee"* is tantamount to deliverance already received. It means, "If I do not deliver you now, I will deliver you at a time that is better than now. You would prefer to be delivered at this future time rather than now if you were as wise as I am."

Promptness is implied in God's promise of deliverance, for a late deliverance is not truly deliverance. "Ah," someone says, "I am in such trouble that if I do not get deliverance soon I will die of grief." Rest assured that you will not die of despair. You will be delivered before you die that way. God will deliver you at the best possible time.

The Lord is always punctual. You never were kept waiting by Him. You have kept Him waiting many times, but He is prompt to the instant. He never keeps His servants waiting one single tick of the clock beyond His own appointed, fitting, wise, and proper moment. *"I will deliver thee"* implies that His delays will not be too long, lest the spirit of man should fail because of hope deferred. The Lord rides on the wings of the wind when He comes to the rescue of those who seek Him. Therefore, be courageous!

Oh, this is a blessed text! But, unfortunately, I cannot carry it to those of you who need it most. Spirit of the living God, come, and apply these rich consolations to those hearts that are bleeding and ready to die!

As I repeat our text, take special note of the words *I* and *thee*: *"Call upon me in the day of trouble: I will deliver thee."* Those two words are threaded together: *"I will deliver thee."* Men would not, angels could not, but God will. God Himself will rescue the person who calls upon Him. Your part is to call;

God's part is to answer. Poor trembler, do you begin to try to answer your own prayers? Why did you pray to God then? When you have prayed, leave it to God to fulfill His own promise. He says, "Do call upon Me, and I will deliver you."

Especially ponder that word *thee*: *"I will deliver thee."* I know what you are thinking, reader. You murmur, "God will deliver everybody, I believe, but *not me*." But the text says, *"I will deliver thee."* It is the person who calls who will get the answer. If you call upon God, He will answer *you*. To *you* He will give the blessing, even to your own heart and spirit, in your own experience. Oh, for grace to take that personal pronoun and apply it personally to our own souls! Oh, to make sure of the promise as though we could see it with our own eyes!

The apostle wrote, *"Through faith we understand that the worlds were framed by the word of God"* (Heb. 11:3). I know beyond the shadow of a doubt that the worlds were made by God. I am sure of it. Yet I did not see Him making them. I did not see the light appear when He said, *"Let there be light"* (Gen. 1:3). I did not see Him divide the light from the darkness and gather the waters together so that the dry land appeared. Yet I am quite sure that He did all this. Even though I was not there to see God make even a bird or a flower, all the evolutionists in the world cannot shake my conviction that God created the world.

Why should I not have the same kind of faith about God's answer to my prayer in my time of trouble? If I cannot see how He will deliver me, why should I wish to see it? He created the world well enough without me being there and knowing how

He would do it, and He will deliver me without my having a finger in it. It is no business of mine to see how He works. My business is to trust in my God and to glorify Him by believing that what He has promised, He is able to perform (Rom. 4:21).

Taking Turns with God

We have had three sweet things to remember, and I will close this chapter with a fourth. It is this: both God and the praying person have parts to play in this process.

That is an odd idea to close with, but I want you to notice it. First, here is your part: *"Call upon me in the day of trouble."* Next is God's part: *"I will deliver thee."* Again, you take another part in that you are delivered and in that you praise Him for it: *"Thou shalt glorify me."* Then, the Lord takes the last part in that He receives the glory. Here is an agreement, a covenant that God enters into with those who pray to Him and are helped by Him. He says, "You will have the deliverance, but I must have the glory. You will pray, I will bless, and then you will honor My holy name." Here is a delightful partnership: we obtain what we so greatly need, and all that God asks is the glory that is due unto His name.

Poor troubled heart! I am sure you do not object to these terms. "Sinners," says the Lord, "I will give you pardon, but you must give Me the honor for it." Our only answer is, "Yes, Lord, that we will, forever and ever."

Who is a pardoning God like Thee?
Or who has grace so rich and free?

"Come, souls," He says, "I will justify you, but I must have the glory for it." And our answer is, *"Where is boasting then? It is excluded. By what law? of works? Nay: but by the law of faith"* (Rom. 3:27). God must have the glory if we are justified by Christ.

"Come," He says, "I will put you into My family, but My grace must have all the glory." And we say, "Yes, that it will, good Lord! *'Behold, what manner of love the Father hath bestowed upon us, that we should be called the sons of God'* (1 John 3:1)."

"Now," He says, "I will sanctify you and make you holy, but I must have the glory for it." And our answer is, "Yes, we will sing this song forever: 'We have washed our robes and made them white in the blood of the Lamb (Rev. 7:14). Therefore, we will serve Him day and night in His temple, giving Him all praise.'"

"I will take you home to heaven," God says. "I will deliver you from sin and death and hell, but I must have the glory for it." "Truly," we say, "You will be magnified. Forever and forever we will sing, *'Blessing, and honour, and glory, and power, be unto him that sitteth upon the throne, and unto the Lamb for ever and ever'* (Rev. 5:13)."

Stop, you thief! Where are you going? Running away with a portion of God's glory? A person who would steal God's glory must be quite a villain! Take, for example, a man who was recently an alcoholic. God has loved him and made him sober, but he takes the credit and is extremely proud of his sobriety. What foolishness! Stop it, mister! Stop it! Give God the glory for your deliverance from the degrading vice, or else you are still degraded by ingratitude.

Take another man as an example. He used to swear, but he has been praying now. He even delivered a sermon the other night, or at least a personal testimony. He has been as proud as a peacock about this. Oh, bird of pride, when you look at your fine feathers, remember your black feet and your hideous voice! Oh, reclaimed sinner, remember your former character, and be ashamed! Give God the glory if you have ceased to use profane language. Give God the glory for every part of your salvation.

"I will deliver thee"—that is your share to receive. But, *"Thou shalt glorify me"*—that is God's share, and His only. He must have all the honor from first to last.

Go out, you saved ones, and proclaim what the Lord has done for you. An aged woman once said that if the Lord Jesus Christ really would save her, He would never hear the last of her praise. Join with her in that resolution. Truly, my soul vows that my delivering Lord will never hear the last of my praise.

I'll praise Him in life, and praise Him in death,
And praise Him as long as He lendeth me breath;
And say when the death-dew lies cold on my brow,
"If ever I loved Thee, my Jesus, 'tis now."

Come, poor soul, you who are in the deepest of trouble—God means to glorify Himself by you! The day will yet come when you will comfort other mourners by telling your happy experience. The day will yet come when you who were outcasts will preach the Gospel to outcasts. The day will yet come, poor fallen woman, when you will lead other sinners to the Savior's feet where you now stand weeping!

You, who have been abandoned by the Devil, whom even Satan is tired of, whom the world rejects because you are worn out and stale—the day will yet come when, renewed in heart and washed in the blood of the Lamb, you will shine like a star in the sky, to the praise of the glory of the grace of God, who has made you to be accepted in the Beloved (Eph. 1:6)!

Oh, desponding sinner, come to Jesus! Do call upon Him, I entreat you! Be persuaded to call upon your God and Father. If you can do no more than groan, groan unto God. Drop a tear, heave a sigh, and let your heart say to the Lord, "O God, deliver me for Christ's sake! Save me from my sin and the consequences of it." As surely as you pray this way, He will hear you and say, "Your sins are forgiven. Go in peace." May it be so for you today, my friend.

Chapter 4

Grace Guaranteed

*And it shall come to pass, that whosoever shall call
on the name of the LORD shall be delivered.*
—Joel 2:32

*And it shall come to pass, that whosoever shall call
on the name of the Lord shall be saved.*
—Acts 2:21

I f we want to understand the full meaning of Joel
2:32, let us first examine the circumstances at the
time when Joel was writing. Vengeance was
coming toward Judah at full speed. The armies of divine justice had been called forth for war. They ran
like mighty men; they climbed the wall like men of
war (Joel 2:7). They invaded and devastated the land,
and they turned the land from being like the Garden
of Eden into a desolate wilderness. All faces grew
pale; the people were *"much pained"* (v. 6). The sun
itself was dim, the moon was dark, and the stars
withdrew themselves; furthermore, the earth quaked,
and the heavens trembled (v. 10).

At such a dreadful time, when we might have least expected it, between the peals of thunder and the flashes of lightning was heard this gentle word: *"It shall come to pass, that whosoever shall call on the name of the LORD shall be delivered."*

Let us carefully read the verse in context:

And I will show wonders in the heavens and in the earth, blood, and fire, and pillars of smoke. The sun shall be turned into darkness, and the moon into blood, before the great and the terrible day of the LORD come. And it shall come to pass, that whosoever shall call on the name of the LORD shall be delivered.
(Joel 2:30–32)

In the worst times that can ever happen, salvation is still available. When day turns to night and life becomes death, when famine rules the land and the hope of man has fled, there still remains in God, in the person of His dear Son, deliverance to all who will call upon the name of the Lord.

We do not know what is going to happen. Looking into the future, I prophesy dark things. Even so, this light will always shine between the clouds: *"Whosoever shall call on the name of the LORD shall be delivered."*

At Pentecost, Peter set this passage in its place as a sort of morning star of gospel times. When the Spirit was poured out upon God's servants, and sons and daughters began to prophesy (Acts 2:16–17), it was clear that the wondrous time had come that had been foretold so long before (Joel 2:28). Then Peter, as he preached his memorable sermon, told the people, *"Whosoever shall call on the name of the Lord shall be saved,"* thus giving a fuller and more evangelical meaning to the word *"delivered."*

"Whosoever shall call on the name of the LORD shall be delivered"—from sin, death, and hell. He will, in fact, be so delivered as to be, in divine language, *"saved"*—saved from guilt, saved from the penalty and the power of sin, saved from the wrath to come.

These present gospel times are still the happy days in which *"whosoever shall call on the name of the Lord shall be saved."* In the year of grace we have reached a day and an hour in which *"whosoever shall call on the name of the Lord shall be saved."* To you, at this moment, is this salvation sent. A dispensation of immediate acceptance was proclaimed at Pentecost, and it has never ceased. Its fullness of blessing has grown rather than dwindled. The sacred promise stands in all its certainty, fullness, and freeness; it has lost none of its breadth or length. *"Whosoever shall call on the name of the Lord shall be saved."*

I have nothing to write about in this chapter except the old, old story of infinite mercy meeting infinite sin; of free grace leading free will into better things; of God Himself appearing to undo man's ruin that he brought on himself; of God lifting man up by a great deliverance. May the Holy Spirit graciously aid me while I write of these things in simple terms.

The Need of All Mankind

First, there is something that every person needs. That something is deliverance, or salvation. It is the requisite of man, wherever man is found. As long as there are people on the face of the earth, there will always be a need of salvation.

If we were to go into a large city, into its alleys and slums, we would think very differently of human need than we do when we simply come from our own quiet homes, step into our pews, and hear a sermon. The world is still sick and dying; it is still corrupted and rotting. The world is a ship in which the water is rising fast, and the vessel is sinking down into the deep of destruction. God's salvation is needed as much today as when it was preached in the days of Noah. God must step in and bring deliverance, or there remains no hope.

In Present Trouble

I have no doubt that many readers need deliverance from present trouble. If you are in much trouble and are very distressed, I invite you to take my text as your guide and believe that *"whosoever shall call on the name of the LORD shall be delivered."* You can be sure that in any form of distress—physical, mental, or whatever it may be—prayer is wonderfully available. As we saw in the previous chapter, God says, *"Call upon me in the day of trouble: I will deliver thee, and thou shalt glorify me"* (Ps. 50:15).

This promise will prove true whenever you come into a position of deep personal distress, whether of a physical kind, a financial kind, or any kind. When you do not know how to act, when you are bewildered and at your wit's end, when wave of trouble has followed wave of trouble until you are like a sailor in a storm who staggers to and fro, if you cannot help yourself because your spirit sinks and your mind fails, call upon God, call upon God, call upon God! Lost child in the woods, with the night fog thickening around you, ready to lie down and die, call upon your Father! Call upon God, troubled one, for *"whosoever shall call on the name of the LORD shall be delivered."*

In the last great Day, when all secrets are known, it will seem unnecessary that people ever spent their time in writing fictional stories, for the real stories of what God has done for those who have cried to Him are infinitely more spectacular. If men and women could just tell in simple, natural language how God has come to their rescue in the hour of imminent distress, they would set the harps of heaven singing with new melodies. They would cause the hearts of saints on earth to glow with new love for God for His wonderful kindness to the children of men. *"Oh that men would praise the LORD for his goodness"* (Ps. 107:8)! Oh, that we could repeatedly remind ourselves of His great goodness during the night of our weeping!

In Future Trouble

Joel 2:32 also promises deliverance from future troubles. What is to happen in the future we do not know. We do know from the Word of God that *"the sun shall be turned into darkness, and the moon into blood"* (v. 31). God will show great wonders in the heavens and in the earth: blood, fire, and pillars of smoke. You will certainly need deliverance then. Fortunately, deliverance will still be near at hand.

God put this encouraging verse in the same chapter as some startling and tragic events in order to advise us that when the worst and most terrible convulsions occur, *"whosoever shall call on the name of the LORD shall be delivered."* The star Wormwood may fall (Rev. 8:11), but we will be saved if we call upon the name of the Lord. Plagues may be poured out, trumpets may sound, and judgments may follow one another as quickly as the plagues of Egypt, but *"whosoever shall call on the name of the LORD shall be delivered."*

While the need for deliverance will notably increase, the abundance of salvation will increase with it. You do not need to fear the direst of all wars, the bitterest of all famines, the deadliest of all plagues, because the Lord has pledged to deliver us if we call upon Him. This word of promise meets the most terrible of possibilities with a sure salvation.

In the Dreaded Last Hour

Yes, when your time comes to die, when to you the sun has turned into darkness, this text ensures deliverance in the dreaded last hour. Call upon the name of the Lord, and you will be saved. Amid the pains of death and the gloom of departure, you will enjoy a glorious visitation, which will turn darkness into light and sorrow into joy. When you wake up amid the realities of eternity, you will not need to dread the Resurrection or the Judgment Day or the yawning mouth of hell. If you have called upon the name of the Lord, you will still be delivered. Though the unpardoned are thrust down to the depths of woe and the righteous are scarcely saved, you who have called upon the name of the Lord must be delivered. The promise stands firm, no matter what may be hidden in the great book of the future. God cannot deny or contradict Himself. He will deliver those who call upon His name.

A Sure Foundation

What is needed, then, is salvation. I do think, beloved believers, that those who preach the Word and long to save souls, need to repeat very often this grand old truth about salvation for the guilty. We need to speak often about deliverance for all who call upon the name of the Lord. Sometimes we talk to friends about the higher life or about attaining high degrees of sanctity. All this is very proper and very good, but still the great fundamental truth is, *"Whosoever shall call on the name of the Lord shall be saved."*

We urge our friends to be sound in doctrine, to be certain about what they believe, and to understand the revealed will of God. This is also very proper. Even so, first and foremost is this elementary, all-important truth: *"Whosoever shall call on the name of the Lord shall be saved."* To this old foundational truth we come back for comfort.

Sometimes I rejoice in the God of my salvation and spread my wings to mount up into communion with the heavenlies. However, there are other seasons when I hide my head in darkness. Then I am very glad for such a broad, gracious promise as this: *"Whosoever shall call on the name of the Lord shall be saved."*

I find that my sweetest, happiest, safest state is that of a poor, guilty, helpless sinner calling upon the name of the Lord and taking mercy from His hands, although I deserve nothing but His wrath. I am happy when I dare to hang the weight of my soul on such a sure promise as this: *"Whosoever shall call on the name of the Lord shall be saved."* No matter who you are, however high your experience, however great your usefulness, you will always need to come back to the same ground on which the poorest and weakest of hearts must stand—the ground of salvation by almighty grace through simply calling upon the name of the Lord.

Prayer: The Means of Deliverance

Now, secondly, let us attentively observe the way in which this deliverance is to be obtained. Help us, blessed Spirit, in this meditation. Deliverance is to be realized, according to Joel 2:32, by calling upon the name of the Lord.

The most obvious meaning of this verse is that we are to pray. Are we not brought to the Lord by a trustful prayer, a prayer that asks God to give the needed deliverance and expects to receive it from Him as a gift of grace?

The words of Joel 2:32 amount to much the same thing as saying, "Believe and live." How can a person call upon God if he has not heard of Him (Rom. 10:14)? And if the person has heard, his calling will be in vain if he does not believe as well as hear.

To *"call on the name of the LORD"* is to pray a believing prayer—to cry to God for His help and to leave yourself in His hands. This is very simple, is it not? There is no cumbersome process here, nothing complex and mysterious. No priestly help is needed, except the help of our Great High Priest, who always intercedes for us (Heb. 7:25). A poor, broken heart pours its distress into the ear of God and calls upon Him to fulfill His promise to help in the time of need—that is all. I thank God that nothing more is mentioned in our texts. The promise is *"whosoever shall call on the name of the Lord shall be saved."*

To the One True God

Although obtaining deliverance is as simple as calling on the name of the Lord, Acts 2:21 contains within it a measure of specific instruction. First, the prayer must be to the true God. Whoever calls on the name of Jehovah will be saved. There is something distinctive here. Suppose one calls on Baal, another on Ashtoreth, and a third on Molech; none of these people would be saved. The promise is specific: *"Whosoever shall call on the name of the Lord* [Jehovah] *shall be saved."*

You know that triune name, "Father, Son, and Holy Spirit." Call upon it. You know how the name of Jehovah is set forth most conspicuously in the person of the Lord Jesus. Call upon Him. Call upon the true God. Call upon no idol, call upon no Virgin Mary, call upon no saint, living or dead. Call upon no impression of your mind! Call upon the living God, upon Him who reveals Himself in the Bible, upon Him who manifests Himself in the person of His dear Son. For whoever calls upon this God will be saved.

You may call upon the idols, but these will not hear you. *"Eyes have they, but they see not: they have ears, but they hear not"* (Ps. 115:5–6). You may call upon mere men to deliver you, but they are all sinners like you. Many call upon priests, but they cannot deliver their most zealous parishioners. But, *"whosoever shall call on the name of the Lord* [Jehovah] *shall be saved."*

Notice that the key is not the mere repetition of a prayer as a sort of charm or a kind of religious witchcraft. You must make a direct address to God, an appeal to the Most High to help you in your time of need. In presenting true prayer to the true God, you will be delivered.

With Intelligence

Moreover, the prayer should be intelligently presented. Let us take a closer look at the words *the name* in the verse, *"Whosoever shall call on the name of the Lord."* Now, by the word *name* is meant the person, the character of the Lord. Therefore, the more you know about the Lord, and the better you know His name, the more intelligently you will call upon that name. If you know His power, you will call upon that power to help you. If you know His mercy, you will call upon that mercy to save you. If you know His wisdom, you will feel that He knows your difficulties and can help you through them. If you understand His immutability, you will call upon the same God who has saved other sinners to come and save you.

It would be wise, therefore, for you to study the Scriptures faithfully and to ask the Lord to manifest Himself to you so that you may know Him. To the degree that you are acquainted with Him, you will be able to call with confidence upon His name.

Little as you may know, call upon Him according to the little that you do know. Cast yourself upon

Him, whether your trouble is external or internal, but especially if it is internal. If it is the trouble of sin, if it is the burden of guilt, if it is a load of horror and fear because of wrath to come, call upon the name of the Lord, for you will be delivered.

Your deliverance is promised by God. The promise is not, "He may be delivered," but, "He *'shall be.'*" Note well the everlasting *"shall"* of God—irrevocable, unalterable, unquestionable, irresistible. His promise stands eternally the same. *"Hath he said, and shall he not do it?"* (Num. 23:19). Yes, He will do what He has said. *"Whosoever shall call on the name of the Lord shall be saved."*

For God's Glory

This way of salvation—calling upon the name of the Lord—glorifies God. He asks nothing of you but that you ask everything of Him. You are the beggar, and He is the Benefactor. You are in trouble, and He is the Deliverer. All you have to do is to trust Him and ask Him. This is easy enough. This takes the matter out of your hands and puts it into the Lord's hands. Do you not like the plan? Put it into practice immediately! It will prove itself gloriously effective.

Dear friends, I am sure I write to some who are under severe trial. You are beginning to lose hope. Perhaps you have given up, or, at any rate, have given yourself up. Yet, I ask you, call upon the name of the Lord. You cannot perish praying; no one has ever done so. If you could perish praying, you would be a new wonder in the universe. A praying soul in hell is an utter impossibility. A man calling on God and rejected by God—the supposition is not to be endured! *"Whosoever shall call on the name of the Lord shall be saved."*

God Himself would have to lie, deny His nature of love, forfeit His claim to mercy, and destroy the integrity of His character if He were to let a poor sinner call upon His name and yet refuse to hear him. There will come a day in the next state when He will say, "I called, but you refused," but that day is not now. While there is life, there is hope. *"To day if ye will hear his voice, harden not your heart"* (Ps. 95:7–8). Call upon God at once, for this guarantee of grace runs through all the regions of mortality. *"Whosoever shall call on the name of the Lord shall be saved."*

I recollect a time when, if I had heard a simple sermon on this subject, I would have leaped into comfort and light in a single moment. Is it such a time with you? I used to think that I must *do* something, that I must *be* something, that I must in some way prepare myself for the mercy of God. I did not know that simply calling upon God, simply trusting myself to His hand, simply petitioning His sacred name, would bring me to Christ the Savior.

However, this is the case, and I was indeed happy when I found it out. Heaven is given away. Salvation may be had for the asking. I hope that many a captive heart will at once leap to loose his own chains and cry, "It is even so. If God has said it, it must be true. There it is in His own Word. I have called upon Him, and I must be delivered."

To Whom Is the Promise Given?

Notice the people to whom this promise and this deliverance are given: *"Whosoever shall call on the name of the LORD shall be delivered."*

Grace Guaranteed

To Those Afflicted by Troubles or Sin

In the book of Joel, the people had been greatly afflicted—afflicted beyond all precedent, afflicted to the very brink of despair. But the Lord had said, *"Whosoever shall call on the name of the LORD shall be delivered."*

Go down to the hospital. You may select, if you wish, a hospital for recovering alcoholics or drug users. In that house of misery, you may stand at each bed and say, *"Whosoever shall call on the name of the Lord shall be saved."* You may then hasten to the jail. You may stop at every door of every cell, yes, even at the bars of the cells on death row, and you may safely say to each one, *"Whosoever shall call on the name of the LORD shall be delivered."*

I know what the Pharisees will say: "If you preach this, people will go on in sin." It has always been true that the great mercy of God has been turned by some into a reason for continuing in sin, but God—and this is the wonder of it—has never restricted His mercy because of that. It must be a terrible provocation of almighty grace when people pervert God's mercy into an excuse for sin, but the Lord has never even taken the edges off His mercy because people have misused it. He has still made His mercy stand out bright and clear: *"Whosoever shall call on the name of the Lord shall be saved."*

Still the Lord cries, "Turn and live." In Isaiah, He puts it this way:

> Let the wicked forsake his way, and the un-righteous man his thoughts: and let him return unto the LORD, and he will have mercy

81

upon him; and to our God, for he will abun-
dantly pardon.   *(Isa. 55:7)*

Undimmed is that brave sun that shines on the foulest trash heaps of evil. Trust Christ and live! Call upon the name of the Lord, and you will be pardoned. Yes, you will be rescued from the bondage of your sin and will be made a new person, a child of God, a member of the family of His grace. Those most afflicted by troubles and those most afflicted by sin are met by this gracious promise: *"Whosoever shall call on the name of the Lord shall be saved."*

To Both Small and Great

Yes, but there were some, according to Joel, who had the Spirit of God poured out upon them. What about them? Were they saved by that? Oh, no! Even those whom God's Spirit enabled to dream dreams and to see visions had to come to the palace of mercy by this same gate of believing prayer: *"Whosoever shall call on the name of the LORD shall be delivered."*

Ah, poor soul! You say to yourself, "If I were a deacon of a church, if I were a pastor, oh, then I would be saved!" You do not understand anything about this matter. Church officers are no more saved by their office than you are by being without office. We owe nothing to our official positions in this matter of salvation. In fact, we may owe our damnation to our official standings unless we carefully watch our ways. Preachers have no advantage over common people. I assure you, I am quite happy to go to Christ on the same footing as any one of my readers, regardless of who he may be.

> Nothing in my hand I bring,
> Simply to Thy cross I cling.

Often, when I have been cheering up a poor sinner and urging him to believe in Christ, I have thought, "Well, if he will not drink this cup of comfort, I will drink it myself." I assure you, I need it as much as those to whom I offer it. I have been as great a sinner as any of you, my readers, and therefore I take the promise for myself. The divine cup of comfort will not be lost; I will accept it.

I came to Jesus as I was, weary, worn, faint, sick, and full of sin. I trusted Him for myself and found peace—peace on the same ground that my texts set before us. If I could drink this consolation, you may drink it, too. The miracle of this cup is that millions may drink from it, yet it is just as full as ever. There is no restriction in the word "*whosoever.*"

You young women who have the Spirit of God upon you, and you old men who dream, it is neither having the Spirit of God nor the dreaming that will save you, but your calling on the sacred name. For, "*whosoever shall call on the name of the Lord shall be saved.*" There are some upon whom the Spirit of God has not fallen. They do not speak with tongues or prophesy the future or work miracles, but though they do none of these marvels, it remains true for them that "*whosoever shall call on the name of the Lord shall be saved.*" Though no supernatural gift is bestowed upon them, though they see no vision and cannot speak with tongues, if they have called upon the name of the Lord, they are saved. The way of salvation is the same for the little as well as for the great, for the poorest and most obscure as well as for the strong in faith who lead the army of God to battle.

To Those without Devout Feelings

"Ah," someone else says, "but I am worse than that. I have no devout feelings. I would give all that I own to have a broken heart. I wish I could feel despair, but I am as hard as a stone."

I have been told that sorrowful story many times, and it is almost always true that those who most mourn their lack of feeling are those who feel most acutely. They say that their hearts are like hardened steel, but it is not true. Even if it were true, *"whosoever shall call on the name of the Lord shall be saved."*

Do you think that the Lord wants you to give yourself a new heart first and that then He will save you? My dear soul, if you had a new heart, you would be saved already and would not need Him to save you. "Oh, but I must have devout feelings!" You must? Where will you go to get them? Are you going to search the trash heap of your depraved nature to find devout feelings there?

Come to God without any devout feelings. Come just as you are. Come, you who are like a frozen iceberg, who have nothing in you whatsoever but that which chills and repels. Come, call upon the name of the Lord, and you will be saved. As someone once wrote, "Wonders of grace to God belong." It is not a small gospel message for small sinners that He has sent us to preach, but ours is a great gospel message for great sinners. *"Whosoever shall call on the name of the Lord shall be saved."*

To Nobodies

"Ah, well," someone says, "I cannot believe that salvation is meant for me; I am a nobody." A nobody, are you? I have a great love for nobodies. I am tired of somebodies, and the worst somebody in the world is my own somebody. How I wish I could always throw my own somebody out and keep company with none but nobodies!

Nobody, where are you? You are the very person that I am sent to look after. If there is nothing in you, there will be all the more of Christ. If you are not only empty, but cracked and broken; if you are done for, destroyed, ruined, and utterly crushed, to you is this word of salvation sent: *"Whosoever shall call on the name of the Lord shall be saved."*

I have opened the gate wide. If the entrance led to the wrong track, all the sheep would go through. But since it is the right road, I can leave the gate open as long as I wish, yet the sheep will evade it unless You, Great Shepherd, go around the field and lead them in. Take up in Your own arms a lost lamb whom You purchased long ago with Your dear heart's blood. Take him upon Your gracious shoulders, rejoicing as You do it, and place him within the field where the good pasture grows.

A Bountiful Blessing

I want you to dwell for a minute on the blessing itself. *"Whosoever shall call on the name of the LORD shall be delivered."* I will not write much more about it because I have explained a good deal about it already.

When a person gives you a promise, it is a very good rule to understand it in the narrowest sense. This is being fair to the person who gives the promise. Let him interpret it liberally if he wishes, but he is actually bound to give you no more than the bare terms of his promise.

Now, this is a rule that all God's people may safely practice: We may always understand God's promises in the largest possible sense. If the words could possibly mean more than you thought at first glance, you may certainly believe the broader meaning. He *"is able to do exceeding abundantly above all that we ask or* [even] *think"* (Eph. 3:20). God never draws a line in His promise so that He may barely go up to it. No, it is with the great God as it was with His dear Son, who, although He was sent *"unto the lost sheep of the house of Israel"* (Matt. 15:24), spent a great part of His time in Galilee, which was called, "Galilee of the Gentiles." Furthermore, as we will see in the next chapter, He went to the very edge of Canaan to find a Canaanite woman so that He could give her a blessing.

Therefore, you may believe the broadest and most generous implications of our text, Joel 2:32, just as Peter did. The New Testament is known for giving a broader meaning to Old Testament words. It does so most properly, for God loves us to treat His words with the breadth of faith.

If you are the object of the wrath of God, if you believe that God's hand has visited you on account of sin, come to God. Call upon Him, and He will deliver you both from judgment and from the guilt that brought judgment—both from the sin and from that which follows the sin. He will help you to escape. Go to Him now.

Perhaps you are a child of God who is in trouble. Perhaps that trouble eats away at your spirit and daily causes your heart to weep. Call upon the Lord. He can take away the vexation and also the trouble. *"Whosoever shall call on the name of the LORD shall be delivered."* On the other hand, you may still have to bear the trouble, but it will be so transformed that it will be a blessing rather than an evil. When the nature of your cross has been changed, you will fall in love with it.

If sin is the cause of your present trouble, if sin has brought you into bondage to evil habits, if you have been a drunkard and do not know how to learn sobriety, if you have been immoral and have become entangled in evil relationships, call upon God. He can break you away from the sin and set you free from all its entanglements. He can cut you loose right now with the great sword of His grace and make you free. Although you feel like a poor sheep between the jaws of a lion, ready to be devoured immediately, God can come and pluck you out of the lion's jaws. The prey will be taken from the mighty, and the captive will be delivered (Isa. 49:24). Only call upon the name of the Lord, and you will be delivered!

The Consequences of Refusing the Blessing

As I conclude this chapter, I must explain one unhappy thought. I want to warn you about the common neglect of this blessing. You would think that everybody would call upon the name of the Lord, but read the second part of Joel 2:32: *"For in mount Zion and in Jerusalem shall be deliverance, as the LORD hath said."* It will be there, as the Lord has said. But will those in mount Zion and Jerusalem receive God's deliverance then? Unfortunately, not all of them will, for notice the last part of the verse: *"And in the remnant whom the LORD shall call."* It seems to leave me altogether speechless, that word *"remnant."* What! Will all not come? No, only a remnant. And even that remnant will not call upon the name of the Lord until God first calls them by His grace. This is almost as great a wonder as the love that so graciously invites them. Will all not call upon His blessed name? No, only a remnant? Are they madmen? Could even devils behave worse? If they were invited to call upon God and be saved, would they refuse?

Unhappy business! The way is plain, but *"few there be that find it"* (Matt. 7:14). After all the preaching and all the invitations and all the breadth of the promise, yet all who are saved are contained *"in the remnant whom the LORD shall call."* Is our text not a generous invitation, the setting open of the door, yes, the lifting of the door off its hinges so that it might never be shut? Yet, *"wide is the gate, and broad is the way, that leadeth to destruction, and many there be which go in thereat"* (v. 13).

There they go, streams of them, hurrying impatiently, rushing down to death and hell—yes, eagerly panting, hurrying, running into one another to descend to that awful gulf from which there is no return! No missionaries or ministers are needed to plead with people to go to hell. No persuasive books are needed to urge them to rush onward to eternal ruin.

The Master never spoke a word that is more clearly proven by observation than this: *"Ye will not come to me, that ye might have life"* (John 5:40). People will attend church, but they will not call upon the Lord. Jesus cries, *"Search the scriptures; for in them ye think ye have eternal life: and they are they which testify of me. And ye will not come to me, that ye might have life"* (vv. 39–40). People will do anything rather than come to Jesus. They stop short of calling upon Him.

Oh, my dear readers, do not let it be so with you! Many of you are saved. I earnestly ask you to intercede for those who are not saved. Oh, that my unconverted readers may be moved to pray! Before you lay down this book, breathe an earnest prayer to God, saying,

> *"God be merciful to me a sinner"* (Luke 18:13). Lord, I need to be saved. Save me. I call upon Your name. Lord, I am guilty. I deserve Your wrath. I cannot save myself. Lord, I need a new heart and a right spirit, but what can I do? I can do nothing. Come and give me both the desire and the ability to do what You want.
>
> Now, from my very soul, I call upon Your name. Trembling, yet believing, I cast myself entirely upon You, O Lord. I trust the blood and righteousness of Your dear Son. I trust Your mercy, Your love, and Your power, as they are revealed in Jesus. I dare to claim this promise of Yours, that *"whosoever shall call on the name of the Lord shall be saved."* Lord, save me now, for Jesus' sake. Amen.

Pray this moment, I entreat you, and you will be saved.

Chapter 5

Pleading, Not Contradiction

She said, Truth, Lord: yet...
—Matthew 15:27

In the narrative about the Syrophoenician woman, have you ever stopped to think about the following two verses: *"Then Jesus went thence, and departed into the coasts of Tyre and Sidon. And, behold, a woman of Canaan came out of the same coasts"* (Matt. 15:21–22)? Notice that as Jesus went toward the coast of Sidon, the woman of Canaan came from the seashore to meet Him. In this way, they came to the same town.

Notice how the grace of God arranges things. Jesus and the seeker had a common attraction. He came, and she came. Her coming from the seacoast of Tyre and Sidon would have been of no use if the Lord Jesus had not also come down to the Israelite border of Phoenicia to meet her. His coming made her coming a success. What a happy circumstance when Christ meets the sinner and the sinner meets his Lord!

Our Lord Jesus, as the Good Shepherd, was drawn to that area by the instincts of His heart. He was seeking for lost ones, and He seemed to feel that there was one to be found on the borders of Tyre and Sidon. Therefore, He had to go that way to find that one. It does not appear that He preached or did anything special on the way there. He left the ninety-nine by the sea of Galilee to seek that one lost sheep by the Mediterranean shore. When He had dealt with her, He went back again to His old places of ministry in Galilee.

Our Lord was drawn toward this woman, but she was driven toward Him. What made her seek Him? Strange to say, the Devil had a hand in it, but I do not give him any of the praise. The truth is that a gracious God used the Devil himself to drive this woman to Jesus, for her daughter was *"grievously vexed with a devil"* (Matt. 15:22). She could not bear to stay at home and see her child in such misery.

Oh, so often a great sorrow drives men and women to Christ, even as a fierce wind compels the sailor to hasten to the harbor! I have seen a daughter's great affliction influence the heart of a mother to seek the Savior. No doubt, many a father, broken in spirit by the likelihood of losing a darling child, has turned his face toward the Lord Jesus in his distress. Ah, my Lord, You have many ways of bringing Your wandering sheep back. You even send the black dog of sorrow and of sickness after them. This dog comes after the sheep, and his growling and barking are so dreadful that the poor lost sheep runs to the Shepherd for shelter.

May God make it so with any reader who has a great trouble at home! If your son is sick, may his sickness be the means of your spiritual health. If your daughter has died, may her death bring about your spiritual life. Oh, that your soul and Jesus may meet today. Your Savior, drawn by love, and your poor heart, driven by anguish—may you in this way be brought together!

Now, you would suppose that since Jesus and the Canaanite woman were seeking each other, the happy meeting and the gracious blessing would easily be brought about. As the old saying goes, "The course of true love never did run smooth." For certain, the course of true faith is seldom without trials.

Here was genuine love in the heart of Jesus toward this woman; here, too, was genuine faith in her heart toward Christ. But difficulties sprang up that we never would have expected. It is for the good of us all that they occurred, but we could not have anticipated them. Perhaps there were more difficulties in the way of this woman than of anybody else who ever came to Jesus in the days of His earthly ministry. I have never read any other passage in which the Savior spoke such apparently rough words as He spoke to this woman of great faith. Did such a hard sentence as the following ever fall from His lips at any other time: *"It is not meet to take the children's bread, and cast it to dogs"* (Matt. 15:26)?

Jesus knew her well, and He knew that she could stand the trial and would be greatly benefited by it. He knew that He would be glorified by her faith throughout all future ages. Therefore, with good reason He put her through the exercises that train a vigorous faith. Doubtless, it was for our sakes that He put her through this test. He never would have exposed her to it had she been a weakling unable to sustain it. She was trained and developed by

His rebuffs. While His wisdom tried her, His grace sustained her.

Now, notice how the incident began. The Savior came to the town, but He was not there in public. On the contrary, He sought seclusion. Mark wrote in his gospel,

> *From thence he arose, and went into the borders of Tyre and Sidon, and entered into an house, and would have no man know it: but he could not be hid. For a certain woman, whose young daughter had an unclean spirit, heard of him, and came and fell at his feet.*
>
> *(Mark 7:24–25)*

Why was He hiding from her? He did not usually avoid the quest of the seeking soul. "Where is He?" she asked His disciples. They gave her no information; they had their Master's orders to let Him remain in hiding. He sought quiet, and needed it, and so they discreetly held their tongues. Yet, she found Him and fell at His feet. Somewhere half a hint had been dropped; she had heard it and followed it until she had discovered the house where the Lord was staying.

That was the beginning of her trial: the Savior was in hiding. But He could not be hidden from her eager search. She was all ears and eyes for Him. Nothing can be hidden from an anxious mother who is eager to bless her child.

Disturbed by her, the Blessed One went out into the street, and His disciples surrounded Him. But she was determined to be heard over their heads. Therefore, she began to cry aloud, *"Have mercy on me, O Lord, thou son of David"* (Matt. 15:22). As He walked along, she still cried out with mighty cries and pleadings until the streets rang with her voice. His whereabouts, which He *"would have no man know"* (Mark 7:24), were proclaimed loudly in the marketplace.

Peter did not like it; he preferred a quiet following. John was very disturbed by the noise; he lost a sentence, a very precious sentence, that the Lord had just uttered. The woman's noise was very distracting to everybody, and so the disciples came to Jesus and said, *"'Send her away'* (Matt. 15:23). Do something for her, or tell her to be gone. She cries after us. We have no peace because of her clamor. We cannot hear You speak because of her pitiful cries."

Meanwhile, she, perceiving that they were speaking to Jesus, came nearer, broke into the inner circle, fell down before Him, worshiped Him, and uttered this plaintive prayer: *"Lord, help me"* (v. 25). There is more power in worship than in noise; she had advanced a step. Our Lord had not yet answered her a single word. He had heard what she had said, no doubt, but He had not said a word to her yet. All that He had done was to say to His disciples, *"I am not sent but unto the lost sheep of the house of Israel"* (v. 24).

That did not prevent her nearer approach or stop her prayer, for then she pleaded, *"Lord, help me."* At length, the Blessed One did speak to her. Greatly to our surprise, it was a rebuff. What a cold answer it was! How cutting—or so it seemed! The Lord answered, *"It is not meet to take the children's bread, and cast it to dogs"* (v. 26).

Now, what would the woman do? She was near the Savior; she had an audience with Him, such as it was. She was on her knees before Him, and He appeared to drive her away! How would she act now?

Here is the point that I wish to make. She would not be driven away. She persevered, she advanced nearer, she actually turned the rebuff into a plea. She had come for a blessing, and she believed that she would have a blessing. She meant to plead for it until she won it. Therefore, she dealt with the Savior in a very heroic manner and in the wisest possible style. She answered Him, *"Truth, Lord: yet the dogs eat of the crumbs which fall from their masters' table"* (Matt. 15:27).

I want every reader to learn a lesson from her behavior: you, like this woman, may win with Christ and hear the Master say to you, *"Great is thy faith: be it unto thee even as thou wilt"* (v. 28).

I have gathered three pieces of advice from this woman's example. First, agree with the Lord, whatever He says. Say, *"Truth, Lord."* Say yes to all His words. Secondly, plead with the Lord. *"Truth, Lord: yet..."* Think of another truth, and mention it to Him as a plea. Say, "Lord, I will not let You go; I must plead with You yet." And thirdly, have faith in the Lord, no matter what He says. However He tries you, still believe in Him with unstaggering faith. Know for certain that He deserves your utmost confidence in His love and power.

Agree with the Lord

My first advice to every heart seeking the Savior is this: agree with the Lord. In the Revised Version we read that she said, *"Yea, Lord"* (v. 27), or, "Yes,

Lord." Regardless of what Jesus said, she did not contradict Him in the least. I like the King James translation, for it is very expressive: *"Truth, Lord."* She did not say, "It is hard," or, "It is unkind," but, "It is true." She said, in essence, "It is true that it is not good to take the children's bread and throw it to dogs. It is true that, compared with Israel, I am a dog. For me to gain this blessing would be like dogs feeding on the children's bread. *'Truth, Lord.'"*

Now, dear friend, if you are dealing with the Lord for life and death, never contradict His Word. You will never come into perfect peace if you are in a contradicting mood, for that is a proud and unacceptable condition of mind. He who reads the Bible to find fault with it will soon discover that the Bible finds fault with him. The same may be said of the Book of God as it is said of its Author: *"If ye...walk contrary unto me; then will I also walk contrary unto you"* (Lev. 26:23–24). I may truthfully say of this Holy Book, *"With the froward* [perverse] *thou wilt show thyself froward"* (Ps. 18:26).

Remember, dear friend, that if the Lord reminds you of your unworthiness and your unfitness, He only tells you what is true. It would be wise to say, *"Truth, Lord."* When Scripture describes you as having a depraved nature, say, *"Truth, Lord."* The Bible describes you as going astray like a lost sheep, and the charge is true. It describes you as having a deceitful heart, and you have such a heart. Therefore, say, *"Truth, Lord."* The Bible says you have no strength and no hope. Let your answer be, *"Truth, Lord."*

The Bible never gives unrenewed human nature a good description, nor does it deserve one. The Bible exposes our corruptions and lays bare our falseness, pride, and unbelief. Do not quibble with God's faithful Word. Take the lowest place, and acknowledge that you are a lost and ruined sinner. If the Scriptures seem to degrade you, do not take offense, but admit that they deal honestly with you. Never let proud nature contradict the Lord, for this will only increase your sin.

This woman took the lowest possible place. She not only admitted that she was like one of the little dogs, but she put herself under the table. She said, *"The dogs eat of the crumbs which fall from their masters' table"* (Matt. 15:27).

Yet, she went even lower than that. You have probably supposed that she referred to the crumbs that fell from the table of the Master Himself. If you will kindly look at the passage, you will see that it is not so. *"Their masters'"* refers to several masters. The word is plural, and it refers to the children who were the little masters of the little dogs. She, in fact, put herself under the children's table, rather than under the Master's table.

Thus, she humbled herself to be not only like a dog to the Lord, but like a dog to the house of Israel—to the Jews. This was going very far indeed, for a Tyrian woman of proud Sidonian blood to admit that the Jews were to her like masters, that these disciples who had just said, *"Send her away"* (v. 23), stood in the same relation to her as the children stand toward the little dogs under the table. Great faith is always the sister of great humility. It does not matter how low Christ put her, she sat there. *"Truth, Lord."*

I earnestly advise every reader of mine to consent to the Lord's verdict. Never argue with the sinner's

Friend. When your heart is heavy, when you think you are the greatest of sinners, remember that you are a greater sinner than you think. Though your conscience has rated you very low, you may go even lower and still be in the right place. For, to tell you the truth, you are as bad as bad can be. You are worse than your darkest thoughts have ever painted you. You are a wretch most undeserving and hell-deserving. Apart from sovereign grace your case is hopeless. If you were now in hell, you would have no cause to complain against the justice of God, for you deserve to be there. If you have not yet found mercy, I fervently desire that you would agree with the severest declarations of God's Word. They are all true, and they all apply to you. Oh, that you would say, "Yes, Lord. I do not have a syllable to say in self-defense!"

Furthermore, if it should appear to your humbled heart to be a very strange thing for you to be saved, do not fight against that belief. A proper sense of divine justice may suggest to you the following thoughts: "What! Me saved? Then I would be the greatest wonder on earth! Surely, God would have to go beyond all former mercy to pardon someone like me. He would be taking the children's bread and throwing it to a dog. I am so unworthy, and so insignificant and useless, that even if I were saved, I would be good for nothing in God's service. How can I expect the blessing?"

Do not attempt to argue to the contrary. Do not seek to magnify yourself. Rather, cry, "Lord, I agree with Your evaluation of me. I freely admit that if I am forgiven, if I am made Your child, and if I enter heaven, I will be the greatest marvel of immeasurable love and boundless grace that ever lived in earth or heaven."

We should be all the more ready to agree with every syllable of the divine Word because Jesus knows us better than we know ourselves. The Word of God knows more about us than we can ever discover about ourselves. We are partial to ourselves, and so we are half blind. Our judgment always fails to hold the balance evenly when our own case is being weighed. What person is not on good terms with himself? Your faults, of course, are always excusable. And if you do a little good, why, it deserves to be talked of and to be valued like diamonds. Each one of us is a very superior person—so our proud hearts tell us.

However, our Lord Jesus does not flatter us. He lets us see our cases as they are. His searching eye perceives the bare truth of things. He is *"the faithful and true witness"* (Rev. 3:14) who deals with us according to the rule of uprightness. Oh, seeking soul, Jesus loves you too much to flatter you. Therefore, I ask you to have such confidence in Him that, however much He may rebuke, reprove, and even condemn you by His Word and Spirit, you may without hesitation reply, *"Truth, Lord."*

Nothing can be gained by contradicting the Savior. Imagine a beggar standing at your door and asking for charity. He goes about it the wrong way if he begins a discussion with you and contradicts your statements. If beggars must not be choosers, certainly they must not be controversialists. If a beggar wants to dispute, let him dispute, but let him give up begging. If he quibbles about how he will receive your gift, or how or what you will give to him, you will probably send him on his way. A critical sinner disputing with his Savior is certainly a fool.

As for me, my mind is made up that I will quarrel with anyone else sooner than with my Savior. I will especially contend with myself and pick a desperate quarrel with my own pride rather than have a shade of strife with my Lord. To contend with one's benefactor is foolish indeed! For the justly condemned to quibble with the Lawgiver, who has the prerogative to pardon, would be folly. Instead of that, with heart and soul I cry, "Lord, whatever I read in the Holy Scriptures, which are the revelation of Your mind, I do believe it, I will believe it, I must believe it. Therefore, I say, *'Truth, Lord.'* It is all true, even if it were to condemn me forever."

Now, notice this: if you find your heart agreeing with what Jesus says, even when He answers you roughly, you may depend on it that this is a work of grace. Human nature is very proud and stands very much upon its silly dignity; therefore, it contradicts the Lord when He deals truthfully with it and humbles it. Human nature, if you want to know its true condition, is that naked thing that so proudly tries to cover itself with apparel of its own devising. See, it sews fig leaves together to make itself clothes! What a destitute object! Clothed with withered leaves, it seems worse than naked! Yet, this wretched human nature proudly rebels against salvation by Christ. It will not hear of imputed righteousness; it believes that its own righteousness is far dearer. Woe to the obstinate pride that rivals the Lord Jesus Christ!

If, my reader, you are of the proper thinking and are willing to acknowledge that you are a sinner, lost, ruined, and condemned, it is well with you. If you are of this attitude—that whatever humbling truth the Spirit of God may teach you in the Word or teach you by the conviction of your conscience, you will agree with it at once and confess, "It is true"—then the Spirit of God has brought you to this humble and truthful and obedient condition. You are going in the right direction.

Plead with the Lord

Our second lesson from the account of the Syrophoenician woman is this: although you must not quibble with Christ, you may plead with Him. She said, *"Truth, Lord,"* but she added, *"yet..."*

Setting One Truth next to Another

When you plead with Christ, do what the Syrophoenician woman did: set one truth next to another. Do not contradict a sad truth, but bring up a happy one to meet it.

Do you remember how the Jews were saved out of the hands of their enemies in the book of Esther? Allow me the tell the story. The king had issued a decree that, on a certain day, the people of his kingdom could rise up against the Jews, slay them, and take their possessions as plunder. Now, according to the laws of the Medes and Persians, this decree could not be altered; it stood firm. What could be done? How was it to be turned around? Why, by meeting that ordinance with another. Another decree was issued stating that although the people might rise against the Jews, the Jews could defend themselves. If anybody dared to hurt the Jews, they could slay him and take his property. One decree thus counteracted another.

How often we may use the holy art of looking from one doctrine to another! If a truth looks dark, it is not wise for me to dwell on it all the time. It is wise to examine the whole range of truth and see if there is not some other doctrine that will give me hope. David practiced this when he said of himself, *"So foolish was I, and ignorant: I was as a beast before thee"* (Ps. 73:22), for he confidently added, *"Nevertheless I am continually with thee: thou hast holden me by my right hand"* (v. 23). He did not contradict himself, yet the second verse removes the bitter taste left by the first. The two sentences together set forth the supreme grace of God, who enabled a poor beastlike being to commune with Him. I beg you to learn this holy art of setting one truth side by side with another so that you may have a fair view of the whole situation and not despair.

For instance, I meet with people who say, "Oh, pastor, sin is an awful thing; it condemns me. I feel that I can never answer the Lord for my iniquities, nor stand in His holy presence." This is certainly true, but remember another truth: *"The LORD hath laid on him the iniquity of us all"* (Isa. 53:6). Also, *"He hath made him to be sin for us, who knew no sin"* (2 Cor. 5:21). Furthermore, *"There is therefore now no condemnation to them which are in Christ Jesus"* (Rom. 8:1). Set the truth of the sin-bearing, substitutionary death of our Lord next to the guilt and curse of sin due to you.

"The Lord has an elect people," someone may be saying, "and this discourages me." Why should it?

Do not contradict that truth; believe it as you read it in God's Word. But hear how Jesus put it:

> *I thank thee, O Father, Lord of heaven and earth, because thou hast hid these things from the wise and prudent, and hast revealed them unto babes.*   *(Matt. 11:25)*

To you who are as weak, simple, and trustful as a baby, the doctrine is full of comfort. If the Lord will save a multitude that no person can number, why should He not save me? It is true that it is written, *"All that the Father giveth me shall come to me"* (John 6:37), but that statement continues, *"And him that cometh to me I will in no wise cast out."* Let the second half of the verse be accepted as well as the first.

Some people are puzzled by the sovereignty of God. We see in Scripture that *"He* [will have] *mercy on whom he will have mercy"* (Rom. 9:18). God may justly ask, *"Is it not lawful for me to do what I will with mine own?"* (Matt. 20:15). Beloved, do not dispute the rights of the eternal God. *"It is the LORD: let him do what seemeth him good"* (1 Sam. 3:18). Do not quarrel with the King, but come humbly to Him and plead with Him in this way: "O Lord, You alone have the right to pardon. Your Word declares that *'if we confess our sins,* [You are] *faithful and just to forgive us our sins'* (1 John 1:9). And You have said that whoever believes in the Lord Jesus Christ will be saved." This pleading will prevail.

When you read, *"Ye must be born again"* (John 3:7), do not be angry. It is true that to be born again is a work beyond your power, for it is the work of the Holy Spirit. Your need of a work beyond your reach may very well distress you, but the same chapter that says, *"Ye must be born again,"* also says, *"God so loved the world, that he gave his only begotten Son, that whosoever believeth in him should not perish, but have everlasting life"* (v. 16). Thus, it is clear that he who believes in Jesus is born again.

Deriving Comfort from a Hard Truth

This brings me to a second remark: draw comfort even from a hard truth. This may seem to contradict the method I have just described for dealing with difficult passages. I do not wish to throw out that method, but this is an even better method. Instead of setting another verse next to the difficult verse, look deeper into the difficult verse itself and derive comfort even from it.

In the translation of Matthew 15:27, the King James Version is very good, but I must confess that it is not quite as true to the woman's meaning as the Revised Version. She did not say, *"Truth, Lord: yet..."* as if she were raising an objection. She actually said, *"Yea, Lord: for..."* I have been using the King James translation up to this point because it expresses the way in which our minds generally look at things. We imagine that we can battle one truth with another, whereas all truths are agreed and cannot be in conflict. Out of the very truth that looks the darkest we may gain consolation.

The Syrophoenician woman said, *"Yea, Lord: for even the dogs eat of the crumbs which fall from their masters' table"* (Matt. 15:27 RV). She did not draw comfort from another truth that seemed to neutralize the first; but as the bee sucks honey from the nettle, so she gathered encouragement from the Lord's severe words: *"It is not meet to take the children's bread, and cast it to dogs"* (v. 26). From His words she derived this comfort: "That is true, Lord, for even the dogs eat the crumbs that fall from their masters' table."

She did not have to turn what Christ had said upside down. She took it as it stood and spied the comfort in it. I earnestly urge you to learn the art of deriving comfort from every statement of God's Word—not necessarily bringing up a second doctrine, but believing that even the present truth that has a threatening aspect is yet your friend.

Do I hear you say, "How can I have hope? For salvation is from the Lord." Why, that is the very reason that you should be filled with hope. Seek salvation from the Lord alone. If it were from yourself, you might despair; but since it is from the Lord, you may have hope.

Do you cry out, "Oh no! I can do nothing"? Why does that matter? The Lord can do everything. Since salvation is from the Lord alone, ask Him to be the Alpha and Omega, the beginning and ending of your salvation.

Do you groan, "I know I must repent, but I am so unfeeling that I cannot reach the right measure of tenderness"? This is true; therefore, the Lord Jesus is exalted on high to give repentance. You will no more repent in your own power than you will go to heaven in your own merit. But the Lord will grant you *"repentance unto life"* (Acts 11:18). For repentance, also, is a fruit of the Spirit.

Beloved, when I was under conviction of sin, I heard the doctrine of divine sovereignty: *"He* [will have] *mercy on whom he will have mercy"* (Rom. 9:18). However, that did not frighten me at all, for I felt more hopeful of grace through the sovereign will of God than by any other way. My reasoning was this: "If pardon is not a matter of human deserving, but of divine prerogative, then there is hope for me. Why should I not be forgiven as well as others? If the Lord had only three elect ones, and these were chosen according to His own good pleasure, why should I not be one of them?" I laid myself at His feet and gave up every hope but that which flowed from His mercy.

Knowing that He would save a multitude that no person could number, and that He would save every soul who believed in Jesus, I believed and was saved. I was fortunate that salvation does not depend on merit, for I had no merit whatsoever. Since it depends on sovereign grace, then I also could go through that door. I felt that the Lord might as well save me as any other sinner. Since I read, *"Him that cometh to me I will in no wise cast out"* (John 6:37), I came, and He did not cast me out.

Rightly understood, every truth in God's Word leads to Jesus, and not one single word drives the seeking sinner back. If you are a fine person, full of your own righteousness, every gospel truth looks black to you. But if you are a sinner deserving nothing from God but wrath, if you confess in your heart that you deserve condemnation, you are the kind of person that Christ came to save. You are the sort of person that God chose before the foundation of the world, and you may come without any hesitation and put your trust in Jesus, who is the sinner's Savior. Believing in Him, you will receive immediate salvation.

Have Faith in the Lord

In any case, whatever Christ says or does not say, have faith in Him. Look at this woman's faith, and try to copy it. Her faith grew in its understanding of Jesus.

The Lord of Mercy

First, she understood Him to be the Lord of mercy. She cried, *"Have mercy on me"* (Matt. 15:22). Have enough faith, dear reader, to believe that you need mercy. Mercy is not for those who think they have merited it. Such people seek justice, not mercy. Only the guilty need and seek mercy. Believe that God delights in mercy, delights to give grace where it cannot be deserved, delights to forgive where there is no reason for forgiveness but His own goodness. Believe also that the Lord Jesus Christ is the incarnation of mercy. His very existence is mercy to you. His every word means mercy. His life, His death, His intercession in heaven, all mean mercy, mercy, mercy, nothing but mercy. You need divine mercy, and Jesus is the embodiment of divine mercy. He is the Savior for you. Believe in Him, and the mercy of God is yours.

The Son of David

This woman also used the title *"son of David"* (v. 22), in which she recognized His manhood and His kingship toward man. Think of Jesus Christ as God over all, blessed forever, He who made heaven and earth and upholds all things by the word of His power (Heb. 1:3). Know that He became man, veiling His Godhead in this poor flesh of ours. He fed as a babe at His mother's breast, He sat as a weary man by the side of a well, and He died with criminals on the cross. He did all this out of love for man.

Can you not trust this Son of David? David was very popular because he went in and out among the people, and he proved himself to be the people's king. Jesus did the same. Also, David gathered a company of men who were very attached to him. When they came to him, they were a broken-down crew; they were in debt and discontented. All the outcasts from Saul's dominion came to David, and he became a captain to them. Likewise, my Lord Jesus Christ is one chosen out of the people, chosen by God on purpose to be a brother to us, a brother born for adversity, a brother who associates with us despite our meanness and misery. He is the friend of men and women who are ruined by their guilt and sin. *"This man receiveth sinners, and eateth with them"* (Luke 15:2). Jesus is the willing leader of a sinful and defiled people, whom He raises to justification and holiness and causes to dwell with Him in glory forever.

Oh, will you not trust such a Savior as this? My Lord did not come into the world to save superior people who think themselves born saints. But Jesus came to save the lost, the ruined, the guilty, the unworthy. Let such come clustering around Him like bees around the queen bee, for He is ordained on purpose to collect the Lord's chosen ones. It is written, *"Unto him shall the gathering of the people be"* (Gen. 49:10).

The Good Shepherd

This believing woman might have been encouraged by another aspect of Christ. Our Lord said to His disciples, *"I am not sent but unto the lost sheep of the house of Israel"* (Matt. 15:24). "Ah!" she must have thought. "He is a shepherd for lost sheep. Whatever His flock may be, He is a shepherd, and He has tremendous compassion for poor lost sheep. Surely I can look to Him with confidence."

Oh, dear reader! My Lord Jesus Christ is a shepherd by office and by nature, and if you are a lost sheep, this is good news for you. There is a holy instinct in Him that makes Him gather the lambs in His arms and causes Him to search out the lost ones who were scattered in the cloudy and dark day. Trust Him to seek you. Yes, come to Him now, and leave yourself with Him.

A Wealthy Master

Furthermore, this woman had a belief of Christ that He was like a wealthy master. She seemed to say, "Those disciples are children who sit at His table, and He feeds them on the bread of His love. He makes them a huge feast, and He gives them heaping portions of food. If my daughter were healed, it would be a great and blessed thing to me, but to Him it would be no more than a crumb from His table." She did not ask to have a crumb thrown to her; she asked only to be allowed to pick up a crumb that had fallen from the table. She did not even ask for a crumb that the Lord had dropped, but for one that the children had allowed to fall. Children are generally great crumb-makers.

I notice in the Greek that, as the original Greek word for *dogs* means "little dogs," so the word for *crumbs* literally is "little crumbs"—small, unnoticed morsels that fall by accident. Think of this woman's faith. To have the devil cast out of her daughter was the greatest blessing she could imagine, yet she had such a belief in the greatness of the Lord that she thought it would be no more to Him to make her daughter well than for a wealthy master to let a little dog eat a crumb dropped by a child. Is that not splendid faith?

Faith in Who Jesus Is

Can you exercise such a faith? Can you believe— you, a condemned, lost sinner—that if God saves you, it will be the greatest wonder that ever was, but that to Jesus, who made Himself a sacrifice for sin, it will be no more than if your dog or cat should eat a tiny morsel that one of your children had dropped from the table? Can you think of Jesus as so great that what is heaven to you will be only a crumb to Him? Can you believe that He can save you easily? As for me, I believe my Lord to be such a Savior that I can trust my soul entirely to Him. I can trust Him without difficulty. And I will tell you something else: if I had the soul of every reader in my body, I would trust them all to Jesus. Yes, if I had a million sinful souls of my own, I would freely trust the Lord Christ with all of them. I would say, *"I know whom I have believed, and am persuaded that he is able to keep that which I have committed unto him against that day"* (2 Tim. 1:12).

Do not suppose that I can write these things because I am conscious of any goodness of my own. Far from it. My trust is in no degree in myself or in anything I can do or be. If I were good, I could not trust in Jesus. Why should I? I should trust in myself. But because I have nothing of my own, I must live by trust, and I rejoice that I may do so.

My Lord gives me unlimited credit at the bank of faith. I am very deeply in debt to Him, and I have resolved to be more indebted still. If I were a million times more sinful than I am, and then had a million souls each a million times more sinful than my own, I would still trust His atoning blood to cleanse me. I would still trust Him to save me. O Christ, by Your agony and bloody sweat, by Your cross and passion, by Your precious death and burial, by Your glorious resurrection and ascension, by Your intercession for the guilty at the right hand of God, I feel that I can rest in You. May all of you, my readers, come to the understanding that Jesus is abundantly able to save.

Have you been a thief? The last person who was in our Lord's close company on earth was the dying thief. "But oh," you say, "I have led an evil life. I have defiled myself with all kinds of evil." But all with whom Christ associates were all once unclean. They confess that they have washed their robes and have made them white in His blood. Their robes were once so foul that nothing but His heart's blood could have made them white.

Jesus is a great Savior, greater than my pen can write. I fail to fully tell His worth, and I would still fail to do so even if I could express heaven in every word and infinity in every sentence. All the words of men and angels could not fully set forth the greatness of the grace of our Redeemer. Trust Him! Are you afraid to trust Him? Then make a running leap into His arms. Dare to do so.

> Venture on Him, venture wholly;
> Let no other trust intrude.

"Look unto me," He says, *"and be ye saved, all the ends of the earth: for I am God, and there is none else"* (Isa. 45:22). Look! Look now! Look to Him alone. As you look to Him with the look of faith, He will look on you with loving acceptance and say to you, as He said to the Canaanite woman, *"Great is thy faith: be it unto thee even as thou wilt"* (Matt. 15:28). You will be saved at this very hour. You will be at peace with God and as restful as an angel. May God grant you this gift for Christ's sake.